The Knowledge Enterprise

Innovation Lessons from Industry Leaders

Second Edition

Series on Technology Management*

Series Editor: J. Tidd (University of Sussex, UK) ISSN 0219-9823

Published

Vol. 18 Perspectives on Supplier Innovation: Theories, Concepts and Empirical Insights on Open Innovation and the Integration of Suppliers
edited by A. Brem (*University of Erlangen-Nuremberg, Germany*) & J. Tidd (*University of Sussex, UK*)

Vol. 19 From Knowledge Management to Strategic Competence: Assessing Technological, Market and Organisational Innovation (3rd Edition)
edited by J. Tidd *(University of Sussex, UK)*

Vol. 20 Bazaar of Opportunities for New Business Development: Bridging Networked Innovation, Intellectual Property and Business
by J. Paasi (*VTT Technical Research Centre of Finland, Finland*), K. Valkokari (*VTT Technical Research Centre of Finland, Finland*), T. Rantala (*VTT Technical Research Centre of Finland, Finland*), S. Nystén-Haarala (*University of Eastern Finland, Finland*), N. Lee (*University of Eastern Finland, Finland*) & L. Huhtilainen (*University of Eastern Finland, Finland*)

Vol. 21 Workbook for Opening Innovation: Bridging Networked Business, Intellectual Property and Contracting
by J. Paasi (*VTT Technical Research Centre of Finland, Finland*), K. Valkokari (*VTT Technical Research Centre of Finland, Finland*), H. Hytönen (*VTT Technical Research Centre of Finland, Finland*), L. Huhtilainen (*University of Eastern Finland, Finland*) & S. Nystén-Haarala (*University of Eastern Finland, Finland*)

Vol. 22 Discontinuous Innovation: Learning to Manage the Unexpected
by P. Augsdörfer (*Technische Hochschule Ingolstadt, Germany*), J. Bessant (*University of Exeter, UK*), K. Möslein (*Universität Erlangen-Nürnberg, Germany*), B. von Stamm (*Innovation Leadership Forum, UK*) & F. Piller (*RWTH Aachen University, Germany*)

Vol. 23 Open Innovation Research, Management and Practice
edited by J. Tidd (*University of Sussex, UK*)

Vol. 24 The Knowledge Enterprise: Innovation Lessons from Industry Leaders (2nd Edition)
by E. Huizenga (*University of Amsterdam, The Netherlands*)

*The complete list of the published volumes in the series can be found at
http://www.worldscientific.com/series/stm

SERIES ON TECHNOLOGY MANAGEMENT – VOL. 24

The Knowledge Enterprise

Innovation Lessons from Industry Leaders

Second Edition

Edward Huizenga

Benthurst & Co
Amsterdam Business School University of Amsterdam, The Netherlands

ICP Imperial College Press

Published by

Imperial College Press
57 Shelton Street
Covent Garden
London WC2H 9HE

Distributed by

World Scientific Publishing Co. Pte. Ltd.

5 Toh Tuck Link, Singapore 596224

USA office: 27 Warren Street, Suite 401-402, Hackensack, NJ 07601

UK office: 57 Shelton Street, Covent Garden, London WC2H 9HE

Library of Congress Cataloging-in-Publication Data
Huizenga, Edward.
The knowledge enterprise : innovation lessons from industry leaders / Edward Huizenga. -- 2nd edition.
pages cm. -- (Series on technology management ; volume 24)
Revised edition of the author's The knowledge enterprise : implementation of intelligent business strategies, published in 2000.
Includes bibliographical references and index.
ISBN 978-1-78326-542-8 (hardcover : alk. paper)
1. Knowledge management. 2. Business planning. 3. Competition. 4. Information technology. I. Title.
HD30.2.H843 2014
658.4'038--dc23

2014030705

British Library Cataloguing-in-Publication Data
A catalogue record for this book is available from the British Library.

Typeset by Stallion Press
Email: enquiries@stallionpress.com

Printed by FuIsland Offset Printing (S) Pte Ltd Singapore

Acknowledgements

Writing a management book is dependent upon corporate storytelling by business leaders. Specifically, for a story of ten years, it is an interesting phenomenon to understand the decision making and change process a company has gone through. I am truly grateful for the openness of all the managers, who were willing to share their ideas, their experiences and their reflections upon the company growth and business innovation.

The process is a journey of commitment, emotions and moments of truths. Throughout the journey of writing this book, we have been able to rely upon the active support of many people: the senior executives and managers of the participating firms who opened their doors to us: Royal DSM, High Tech Campus Eindhoven, Newtricious, and Janssen Pharmaceutical companies of Johnson & Johnson; the sponsors, my colleagues and MBA students from the Amsterdam Business School. Special thanks must also go to the many contributors and reviewers of this book, and to Eliane Lauwers, Kris Sterkens, Ludo Lauwers, Sonja Willems, Jeroen De Rycker, Rob van Leen, Marcel Wubbolts, Leo Smit, Cees Admiraal, Jérôme Verhagen, Alan Muller, Luis del Villar and Erick Morillo for their subliminal sessions. Special thanks to Friso den Hertog, my master teacher, who taught me the art of innovation. Thanks for sharing your stories, the challenges and for all valuable recommendations. Thanks to the Altuïtion crew, being the engagement engineers who are currently redesigning the customer experience strategies of many companies. Thanks to the members of Holland Food Camp, the people who share the passion for boosting the business. Special thanks to all the guys from the Goesting Culinary Club; thanks for the great seduction of good food, strong chef discipline to make it happen in the kitchen, the great wine and good socializing moments.

And special thanks to my dear friends and family.

This book feels like I have been on an emotional journey. In a journey we judge our total experiences almost entirely on how the emotions appeared at the peak of the journey and how they appeared at the end of the journey. It is a journey similar to a journey in professional sports such as the Tour de France. But for sure, these journeys have one thing in common: when you are on the top of your goal it gives a "performance endorphin high" and a feeling of well-being.

Enjoy the journey.

Edward Huizenga

About the Author

Dr. Edward Huizenga is partner at a strategy consulting firm, Benthurst & Co. He specializes in strategy realization, marketing strategy, customer excellence, process improvement, innovation and (new) business development.

Edward started his career at the Maastricht University in 1998. After studying he worked for years in strategy consulting and as a business development manager in knowledge-intensive, highly professional, high-performance organizations. He is driven by results, and designs and delivers growth strategies and builds bridges between the international academic and business network.

His client engagement is at board-room level with the top-100 companies to achieve breakthroughs in strategy and business innovation. Together with companies he initiates innovation and growth opportunities. His management and consulting expertise includes corporate and business strategy, organization of innovation, new business development, customer experience marketing, the effectiveness of product development and business modeling.

In 1996 Edward obtained an MA in economics from the University of Maastricht and an MA in business administration from Universidad de Zaragoza, and in 2001 a PhD in innovation management from the University of Maastricht. He is the author of numerous management bestsellers such as *Innovation Management — How Frontrunners Stay Ahead* (Edward Elgar Publishing, 2004), *The Knowledge Factor* (with Prof. Dr. J.F den Hertog, Kluwer, 1997) and *The Knowledge Enterprise*, First Edition (with Prof. Dr. J.F den Hertog, Imperial College Press, 2000).

Next to his consulting position he is affiliate associate professor at the Amsterdam Business School, University of Amsterdam, one of Europe's major comprehensive universities. He teaches the executive MBA on marketing strategy with great enthusiasm. He enjoys inspiring the next generation of MBA students who will be future entrepreneurs and business leaders.

He currently lives in the Netherlands with Carine and his three children Lauren, Olaf and Victor. He has a passion for haute cuisine and takes a pleasure in cooking and designing dishes. Being a sports fanatic he is, of course, an active pro race cyclist, regularly challenging the famous French mountains.

Contents

Chapter 1

The Knowledge Enterprise — Organizing for Engagement and Business Innovation

A New Stage of Innovation

Let's think back and consider what has happened to many corporations. Many have evidently transformed their business models to align with changing market circumstances and technological conditions, but which companies actually thrive on innovation in a consistent way? And what characterizes these companies? This book is about the companies' stories behind these remarkable innovations. Innovation is more than just research and development (R&D). European industry leaders take up the challenge to move their industry boundaries: a large corporation that produces and distributes a basic product like eggs has recently transformed into a nutritional and life sciences company. Pharmaceutical firms now delve into the world of the unmet medical needs that patients are waiting for. Chemical firms have moved into growth markets of life and material sciences. Nowadays leading firms deliver innovative solutions that nourish, protect and improve the lives of people, e.g. in areas of food production, medical devices, pharmaceuticals, alternative energy and bio-based materials. Such transformations lift the company to a new stage of innovation. High-tech organizations have evolved into a network organization of over 100 companies, concentrated in a hub, and sharing and exploiting their high-tech competencies. The power of these enterprises rests upon their ability to transform their business model and manage the horizon of successive transformations. This power is rooted in one common driver: the primary role of business innovation. Things truly have changed over the past ten years and these investments in innovation have delivered clear results. Award-winning innovations concerning the nutritional value of eggs lead to a breakthrough in preventive healthcare. Innovations in material sciences now help to provide high-value sports gear for the Olympic Games. An open innovation campus results in the "smartest region of the world."

Everyone agrees that innovation is important, and many companies proclaim that they are assigning top business priority to innovation and customer value. Corporations have learned that the ability to adapt and respond is now as important as the ability to anticipate and act. What can we learn from the innovation practices of industry leaders? And how do thought leaders and global market leaders transform their knowledge organization in search of breakthroughs and revenue-generating new business? First of all, companies have to accept the inflation rate of their competitive position and their core competencies. A competitive position based on unique knowledge and competencies becomes obsolete over time. Competition in mass markets, commoditization, faster time-to-market, eroding margins, loss of patent positions, and new distribution channels have drastically changed the business landscape. The board of the knowledge enterprise is expected to divide attention over an increasing number of important matters. Rebalancing the business portfolio by acquisitions and divestures, cost leadership and operational excellence requires a great deal of management attention. New management topics have appeared, including the rise of customer excellence, open innovation and business models. The bottom line is that, over the past five years, most organizations have invested a great deal of time in streamlining processes, finding new business opportunities, and adapting to changing economic conditions. The organizational focus has transformed from a product and market focus towards a customer focus (Gulati and Oldroyd, 2005) and attention paid to health, welfare, personal care, sustainability etc. (Funk, 2003). These are the new domains for growth. The market needs pertaining to healthcare, food and nutrition are no longer local developments but have a worldwide impact. Organizations that have incorporated these themes into their missions and visions are engaged with societal developments. Becoming an engaged organization requires organizational changes, and demands a thorough questioning of the current business model.

Companies that have taken this route of engagement have transformed themselves. Companies serving markets throughout Europe, Asia and the US stand testament to a number of remarkable results. A range of insightful corporate stories about the transformation of organizations that thrive on customer focus, societal engagement, addressing unmet customer needs and partaking in collaborative innovation are presented in this book. We present the innovation story of Janssen Pharmaceutical companies of Johnson & Johnson in the pharmaceutical industry (Chapter 5), and the corporate transformation story of Royal DSM (Chapter 3), industry leader in the life and material sciences. We describe the story of the "smartest region of the world," as represented by the business model strategy of High Tech Campus Eindhoven (Chapter 4). A close look at corporate entrepreneurship is presented under the guise of the story of the European market leader in the production and distribution of egg products, Newtricious (Chapter 4), a company that has transformed into a knowledge enterprise in the food nutrition and life sciences segment. We examine the organization of innovation and we consider the worldwide innovation strategies (Chapters 6 and 7). We learn about the organizational power of the lateral organization and its execution, and investigate the campus strategy for innovation.

Agility and innovation — seizing new business throughout economic tides

The current economic crisis is like a storm raging at once over all continents of the world. Just like with bad weather, it is possible to take measures that will limit the damage from economic low pressure; you can build your firm on foundations so strong that the basic structure will remain intact. Some firms have learned their lessons with this metaphorical bad weather in the past, and moved over to markets where they can stand up to the wind. Others have invested in the strengthening of their organizational structures, or have decided to abandon vulnerable parts. But what can be done when, suddenly, your firm is hit by unexpected economic conditions? There is, however, also a more positive side to these bad times. Historians show that the best deals are made during crisis periods, because companies' competitors are making mistakes, disappear, or can be acquired for little money. The same goes for suppliers and customers. New windows of opportunity can open in uncertain times. The firms that survive the turmoil will of course have to be aware that the world will be different when the gale has calmed down. In this book we will look at how firms have prepared for and survived several economic tides, primarily by means of innovation (Chapter 6).

Further we will consider what must be done to a company's organizational structure in order to allow growth by innovation (Chapter 7). Dow Chemical's CTO (chief technology officer) William Banholzer (2010), for example, underlines that cyclic firms such as his need to have management strategies installed to guarantee both the customers' needs in the present, and the shareholders' interest in the future. McKinsey consultants Lowell and Farell (2008) tell us what we know and don't know about the effects of the financial crises, namely that companies which nurture flexibility, awareness, and resiliency are more likely to survive the crisis, and even to prosper during it. Meanwhile, Amit and Zott (2012) argue that companies' primary focus should be on business model innovation, since this is where the greatest benefits can be reaped. In order to survive in competition, making improvements to product quality, delivery readiness or production scale is not sufficient. It is important to innovate in areas where the competition does *not* act.

Organizations must quickly and continuously asses their business and the value chain positions that are vulnerable and those that are defensible, and the emerging business areas that make strategic sense. The Boston Consulting Group colleagues Rhodes and Stelter (2009) describe the repertoire of measures that enable firms both to stabilize their business, and to seize new opportunities. "It is all about agility," says London Business School professor Donald Sull (2009). Rawson *et al.* (2013) argue in *Harvard Business Review* that transformations are effective when driven by customer centricity and customer experience. Shifting organizational processes, culture and mindsets to a customer-journey orientation is strategic and transformational. Journey-based transformations are not easy, and they may take years to perfect. But it is the end-to-end customer journey that really counts. You would like to understand your customers more deeply and understand their unconcious motivations and minds (Zaltman, 2003). Rigby *et al.* (2009) argue that in times of crises, in many firms innovation falls into a vulnerable position and becomes the victim of short-term thinking and unwise cost cutting. The decisions are made by analytic "left brain leaders." Firms need "both brain" management: management by pairs of powerful executives with complementary creative and analytic styles. Surviving a recession demands more than either a defensive effort of cost cutting or an aggressive quest for new business. Real survivors are involved in both: careful improvement of operational processes and clearly focussed new investments and reinventing of their business (Gulati *et al.* 2010; Nunes & Breene, 2011).

Innovation is, in a sense, a tacit process; difficult to grasp and measure and even more difficult to manage in a corporation (Drucker, 1998). Its value is recognized if it creates growth and new revenue streams and profits. But if these are not present, or results take a long time and serious resource commitments, its relevance might be questioned. Why would a company, being a market leader, still invest in innovation if the process is risky or unpredictable, and returns on investments take time?

Once again the message is clear. Competitive pressures have pushed business model innovation onto CEOs' priority lists: innovation, customer centricity, societal engagement and business model transformation are the answers for a company striving for growth. This requires the creation of new connections within the organization and connections with customers, other enterprises, societal stakeholders and knowledge institutions. This book provides an overview of current managerial practices of the knowledge enterprise. Each company is an intriguing story about growth, surviving economic tides, innovation strategies, decision making, and tapping into the best science in the world. Senior executives have been confronted with a more profoundly uncertain business environment. Uncertainty surrounds not only the short-term business horizon, but also the future of a global corporation. Much can be learnt from the five innovation rules of Janssen Pharmaceutical companies of Johnson & Johnson. We also consider the seven principles guiding R&D and emerging business areas at DSM and the open innovation practices of High Tech Campus Eindhoven and Newtricious.

Business Innovation — Change the Game, Engagement and Customer Centricity

The new businesses we observed with the companies range from incremental to industry game changing. Some simply enhance the current business and core competencies. They are more or less sustaining innovations as mentioned by Christensen *et al.* (2002) or the "adjacent" business innovations described by Nagji and Tuff (2012). But many others are of a different nature and become more disruptive, or transformational. Business innovations are transformational if they develop new products, new services, new processes and knowledge assets, create new markets and fulfill unmet customer needs. It is about developing breakthroughs and inventing solutions for unmet (customer) needs and emerging markets. Binns *et al.* (2014) even speak of the art of renewal. The key often lies in strategic realization: a set of practices that can guide leaders into a new era of innovation by building strategy, experimentation and execution into the day-to-day routines of the organization.

In his ground-breaking book on the U-theory, Otto Scharmer (2009) reflects upon what companies actually create and how they pay attention to what they create. In his theory of moving through the U-process, companies learn to leave past patterns, connect to the essential "sensing" stage, and arrive at the "crystalizing" stage of vision, intention and finally the "performing" stage of engagement. Companies are able to shift their awareness to allow them to connect with the best future possibility, and to realize it.

The consequences of these innovations have a long-lasting impact, as they require a new business model. Sometimes the corporation needs to orchestrate this business model in a separate business unit in order to nurture and support the emerging business area. But others evolve in a collaborative, open environment or by means of venturing and boosting entrepreneurship in an innovation hub. This book will take you through the business patterns of these corporations, supported by short cases and practical company examples.

One remarkable commonality is that each of the participating companies constantly questioned its existing business model and has consequently transformed over the years. The company stories provide a deeper understanding of this transformation process, which, in reality, is easier said than done. It is the corporate process in finding answers to the question: are we doing the right things (right) for a sustainable future? Sustainability's next frontier is tackling the significant issues that lie at the heart of competitive advantage and long-term viability of the business model of the firm. Many companies struggle to match the sustainability concerns, e.g. trial-and-error projects on environmental friendliness, window dressing on engagement to society needs and communications on transparency. At first glance, this might not strike as particularly significant. In Chapters 4 and 5 we will observe companies setting for themselves a standard of consistent performance that no other industry competitor achieves. Moreover, we have found evidence that the strategy process includes the ability of management to bring their organization into a modus of transformation. How do knowledge enterprises transform and succeed on sustainability and a viable business model through innovation? In an industry and economic setting characterized by rapid change, full of immense threats and opportunities, these companies understand the game-changing rules. These companies know the impact of change on the business model and they cannot afford being exposed to unforeseen events. The insightful and intriguing perspectives from the business cases show how to take actions within the organization.

The creation of a sustainable growth path is driven by companies that rethink their current business model. These companies question their current business, scout emerging business areas and above all rethink and reinvent the industry boundaries.

This calls upon a new kind of innovation in companies, in terms of search for radical, breakthrough, disruptive, or game-changing innovation. The consequences, in terms of risk and financial returns, require the corporation's willingness and senior commitment to explore (unfamiliar) assets and building of new competencies. It also requires an ambition, a company credo as a guideline to build competencies that are rooted in deeper understanding of unmet customer needs. But the willingness to source the quest for new technologies that have no direct business evidence (yet), and to develop emerging market areas is also required.

In this roadmap companies learn to collaborate with stakeholders in the value chain and even more in unidentified markets to address issues on health, aging society and, for example, bio-based challenges. Firms start to make sustainability based models for innovation. For example, agricultural firms enter the knowledge domain of pharmaceuticals; high-tech firms and chemical companies become solution providers in healthcare domains inspired by a brand promise for a better living. In this respect these companies are regenerating their corporate strategy, driven by innovation. Firms are aware of the need to develop new competencies and knowledge in respect of the increasing agility of technology and market dynamics. Their growth strategies are driven by several competency drivers (Johnson *et al.*, 2009; Prahalad & Venkatraman, 2000; Zott & Amit, 2008):

- The strategic foresight, answering the ultimate question "are we doing the right things (right) for the future?"
- The ability to act — investments and divestments in their competencies and market portfolio.
- An enduring commitment to innovation and a long-term perspective for the transformation of their core competencies.
- Design a lateral organizational structure and accompanying organizational process to transform and scout emerging and sustainable growth areas.
- Customer centricity, keeping in mind the unmet customer needs and society trends.

Successful companies show the ability to question their revenue model and the competency of lateral thinking in their organization, that is, thinking beyond the boundaries of one's own organizational domain. This could take form of changing, in some fundamental way, the rules in a long-standing industry like the pharmaceutical sector. Or even redrawing the technological boundaries through an open innovation hub. Or even creating an entirely new industry domain with new added value propositions like nutritional ingredients for remedies on chronic diseases.

Customer centricity is the key driver and ambition of many companies, but what is actually needed to make this a corporate driver on innovation for many companies? This is a driver which is often anchored in a mission statement, the corporate credo, the aspirations and brand positioning statements. Such descriptions show the company's efforts in terms of:

- Creating an impact in people's lives.
- Solving unmet medical needs.
- Discovering the ultimate nutritional value of agricultural products.
- Finding curative and preventive solutions for diseases.
- Creating an impact in the health and wellness of people.

The Lateral Organization

The role of customer needs is accompanied by the commonality that most companies have preserved a hybrid structure for innovation. Streamlining has become a steady organizational practice, and nobody is willing to digress on this. At the same time organizations still need to rely on programming their knowledge development, especially as a way to ensure the correct balance between long-term, fundamental research and short-term, business-driven R&D. One step in this direction is the lateral organization. This seems to be the effective model for seizing the benefits for knowledge-development activities in high-performing organizations (Hertog & Huizenga, 2000). The art of lateral thinking and correct use of lateral organization to ensure knowledge flows is mastered by DSM, Janssen Pharmaceutical companies of Johnson & Johnson, Newtricious and High Tech Campus Eindhoven. Many lateral structures are present in these organizations, such as heavyweight project teams, venture teams, strategy and innovation councils, to name but a few. In particular these organizational structures contributed to transforming the organizations from product- or technology-push companies towards:

- Incorporating unmet customer needs.
- A more sophisticated orientation towards societal developments.
- Leveraging new business and investments in R&D.

Over the past ten years many companies have further decentralized R&D to ensure a closer market connection. At the same time they have implemented cross-organizational structures to align short- and long-term R&D objectives. In this context, a next level of business development has appeared; namely that collaborative innovation is not merely a trend, but is here to stay. New collaborative approaches are constantly appearing, such as open campus models, open innovation partnerships and explicit venturing models with which to seize emerging technologies. Firms are once again investing effectively in the organization to ensure internal and external collaboration and maximum gain from knowledge synergy.

The Knowledge Enterprise — The Creation and Power of Value

This book considers the main transformations of enterprises over the past five years. In particular the focus is on companies that invested in innovation and understand that preoccupation with operational excellence will not be the route for growth; companies that stick to their business model can only excel by improving business efficiency. This strategy of operational excellence is merely distributing the products and services to customers and cost-effectively producing these goods and services. However many companies strive for customer excellence and invest in a roadmap for high-value servicing of their customers (Birkinshaw *et al.*, 2011). These firms adhere to better understanding their customer needs and market trends and, in doing so, address the importance for innovation and the increasing knowledge intensity of business. The managerial challenge that enterprises are facing was illustrated by one of the CEOs of the companies featured in this book:[1]

> A higher added value of products and services, it's all about that management phenomena. Of course the traditional factors of prices and quality matter, but companies will not grow in the end if they do not rethink their business model. In the last ten years markets have become global, competitors are crossing market boundaries and products can be copied rapidly. This means that companies have to ask themselves "are we doing the right things (right)?" Innovations and business development have become a continuous, core business process. The question is how companies are equipped with this challenge.

This vision is supported by many boardroom discussions. But, behind this vision, is the quest for a fundamental change of business activities. It is similar to the economics of inflation: the law of value erosion. The added value of the current business model is declining and this puts pressure on the key revenue drivers. Fighting the law of value erosion is not a one-off decision by the board, which is implemented within a short-time horizon. These kind of value transformations take time, not one year, not two years, but periods of up to five years. It is true that product life cycles have become shorter, time-to-market of new products is speeding up, products become obsolete and services are the vehicle for added value. The business reason for this is

[1] All unreferenced quotes are taken from interviews held with the respective companies at their company headquarters during 2012 and 2013.

evident; the economic drivers of value creation by a company are at stake.

Value Creation

The continuous search for new sources of value is a basic remedy for value erosion. Innovation of products and services is one of the main routes towards the creation of new value. However, the business landscape is changing continuously too, urging firms to rethink their ways of innovating.

Innovating used to look much like launching a rocket to the moon. Years of careful preparation culminate in those two crucial moments: the lift off and the landing; the launching site and the target are given; technology and proper market research offered all the solutions. Talking about innovation was talking about technology push and market pull. No simple talk, but surveyable.

Nowadays, however, our views on innovation have drastically changed. We are becoming aware that product or service innovation are not the only sources for new value. Value can be generated along the whole internal and external value chain, even along foreign value chains. Firms therefore have to develop the capability to find out how (Sawhney & Parikh, 2001) economic value behaves. In order to do this firms must go outside the company's frontiers; go into the open and find new business and margin in the value chains and networks, closest to the customer. They must also go where new consumer needs are emerging (Eyring *et al.*, 2011). In this sense, innovation becomes a continuous quest for better business — namely business innovation. Many firms have understood this and have thus been reinventing their *business models* in a fundamental way (Johnson *et al.*, 2009).

In the quest for new value the business landscape is transforming itself constantly. Often innovations and new strategies are not enough anymore, and the firm (Normann, 2001) has no option other than to "reframe" itself. This is the time for deep strategic change and finding the next core business (Zook, 2007). One must question the company's revenue model or look for growth areas, both of which are easier said than done. Also demanded is a preoccupation with operational excellence, customer processes, distribution channel management, and the alignment of sales with marketing. Further, a company must keep focus, understand the market, deliver quality and slim down. Throughout Europe, Asia and the US this has undeniably led to a number of results. Quality and productivity have been improved. Companies are able to do things quicker and faster using more technology and fewer people. Consequently, price and quality have become preconditions for market positions.

The future of companies will depend more and more on the ability to convert knowledge about customer needs into value propositions and good currency. Firms will have to evolve in this process and innovation is a key to the future growth of the companies. The preoccupation with just providing budget for R&D, developing technology or core products, and then distributing them to the market is now too simplistic. The rules of the game have changed.

New ideas and start-up companies appear which either create new markets or reset the market boundaries. Examples of this are cheaper ways to generate solar energy such as chip technology which improves solar panels efficiency by 20%, water purification systems that use bio-based fuel, isolation materials produced from crop rest of rice production, tomato extracts that are a key ingredient for new medication. What is new and ground-breaking these days becomes common practice within a short time period. Today's organizations are facing a gradual, creeping change, but at the same time a fundamental and irreversible one. The danger of creeping changes is that one gets used to them, just like one gets used to certain small annoyances and gradually accepts the existence of them. At a later stage a reflection opens up one's mind about the gradual changes. One day we won't remember the starting point, the past when there was a time these ideas did not exist.

The story is still unfolding. Market, market segments and distribution channels are key words in the traditional discipline of innovation. It is important to learn about the customers' deep, unconcious needs and preferences. This has even progressed further into the demand for a deep understanding of the customer's mind.

Innovation is about Sustainability — Corporate Motivation to Make a Difference to the World

The remarkable news is that more and more companies blend their innovation and business thinking with sustainability motives. Recent examples include those ranging from impactful eco initiatives and programs that give access to medicine in collaboration with NGOs such as ColaLife (ColaLife is using the Coca-Cola supply chain to get local coverage for medication), to far-reaching programs and technological discoveries, and show a new wave of company developments and innovations. Innovations such as these, amongst countless others, are dedicated to defying the world's economic and social problems.

Healthcare, safety, well-being and nutrition all, of course, play an important role in people's lives. At the same time, however, they also play an important role in today's innovations pursued by many companies. The companies that feature in this book have defined their missions in terms of making a difference in one's personal health and well-being by creating innovative solutions. Many companies conduct R&D activities in order to:

- Find answers to the global demographic shift of wealth from West to East and from North to South, as well as a trend towards an increasingly aged, increasingly urban, increasingly connected, and increasingly wealthy global population.
- Contribute to a growing interest in finding solutions to the societal questions of prevention of (chronic) diseases, curative health and wellness topics.
- Further food, nutrition and food security and enable the availability of the right amount and quality of food.

Example: Easy technology makes a difference — the story of Liter of Light and the Solar Bottle Bulb

Liter of Light is a global open source movement with the aim of providing an ecologically and economically sustainable source of light, especially to those underprivileged households that do not have access to electricity or are unable to afford it. The invention is relatively simple. It involves filling a 1.5 liter plastic bottle with purified water and bleach and installing it onto the roof of a house. The water inside the bottle refracts the sunlight during the daytime and creates the same intensity as a 55-watt light bulb. With the correct installation and materials a solar bottle such as this can last up to five years. As the light relies on the sun it cannot be used at night and is only meant to provide light to buildings and homes during daylight hours.

The idea of using plastic bottles for capturing daylight was first pioneered by Alfredo Moser from Brazil in 2001. Using the technology as a social enterprise it was first launched in the Philippines under the MyShelter Foundation in April 2011. In order to help the idea grow substantially, the Foundation implemented a "local entrepreneur" business model, where bottle bulbs are put together and installed by local people who in return earn a small income for their work. In 2011 the technology behind Liter of Light was developed by students from the Massachusetts Institute of Technology (MIT). The initiative was based on the concept of "Appropriate Technologies" — namely to provide simple and easily replicable technologies to communities in need.

PepsiCo has since formed a partnership with the MyShelter Foundation Liter of Light project. PepsiCo's involvement resulted in the installation of used plastic Pepsi bottles on roofs to refract sunlight. This cuts down electric bills and helps to reduce carbon emissions. The PepsiCo brand helped by means of volunteer action, online donation, direct sponsorship and training. In consequence, over 20,000 lights were installed. In order to help develop the project, PepsiCo established a center to train volunteers and educated companies, schools and people on how to create and install lights. The project was commended at the 2011 World Climate Conference. Further information about this project can be found at www.aliteroflight.org.

The common denominator for these industry-leading companies is sustainable innovation, contemporaneously with its search for new discoveries at the crossing borders of high-performance materials, food, life sciences and pharmaceuticals.

Transforming the Business Models, Orchestration and Collaborative Innovation

Over the past five years, a large number of firms have worked hard to target the development of new products and services to the market place. They were forced to increase the development speed, enhance the quality of products and services, and cater for today's customer demands. In doing so, attention has shifted from radical "novel" innovation to incremental innovation. It is becoming clear now, however, that this development has moved too far to the defensive side of things. It is important to remember that firms should be concerned not only with today's market, but with tomorrow's market as well; firms should not be concerned with today's market share, but with the creation of mindshare (that is, understanding how customers think and how to gain the essential insights into the mind of the market (Zaltman, 2003)). Today's successful innovations are usually based on perishable breakthroughs (Christensen, 1997; Christensen *et al.*, 2002). This was the conclusion made by small, large and network enterprises in order to speed ahead for pharmaceuticals, high-tech or nutritional food. This insight is gaining recognition in firms that wish to be (or continue to be) at the forefront. Long ago Hamel and Prahalad (1994) talked about *Strategy by Stretch* and Jim Collins (2001) about *Good to Great*; essentially firms gearing for targets that challenge its employees to accomplish what is virtually impossible. There is hardly one sector of industry in which similar major challenges are lacking. This has changed the business models of many companies:

- Pharmaceutical companies do not provide medicines anymore but are caring for patients.
- Agricultural companies are developing high-end specialties to create a better living for people and concern about the nutrition and health patterns of poor people.
- Chemical companies transform from bulk to specialties. They even take a direct marketing strategy to customers, such as investing in brand awareness by painting the favelas of Rio

de Janeiro in order to improve the life of poor people in the suburbs of the major city communities.
- Media companies become knowledge providers in family cooking, design of beautiful dishes and grasping the food facts and chef's cuisine recipes, e.g. 24Kitchen.
- LEGO, the popular toy manufacturer, uses customer feedback, crowd sourcing (Design byME) and invites the customer into the product development team with Mindstorms.

Knowledge is the most important fuel for value creation in firms and institutions. Competitive advantage becomes increasingly based on exclusive knowledge, or in action perspective: core competencies. At the same time, the development of knowledge is gaining momentum. Knowledge is becoming obsolete and imitated more quickly, while its complexity continuously rises. The firm has prepared itself for the continuous development, acquisition, integration, storage and retrieval of knowledge. The firm has to be rebuilt as a knowledge system, a knowledge system in which crucial and risky choices have to be made, or in other words: a *knowledge enterprise.* This is about making risky choices. It means that we have to be able to answer the following basic questions:

- What is the knowledge ambition?
- Which knowledge and competencies does the firm posses?
- Why is R&D and business innovation vitally important for a firm's competitive advantage?
- How do companies organize business innovation and in which fields do companies want to be first, catch up, or take a lead?

All these questions are concerned with the starting point of the knowledge enterprise: the *knowledge ambition*. This book delves into the strategic challenge of companies that commit to this journey for higher value. We provide an in-depth view of the route of companies such as these in their quest for changing their business model. These companies have one thing in common: a deep commitment to innovation and transformation.

Transformation of the business model

What makes these companies special? What makes them a knowledge enterprise? These companies think differently, they challenge their own business model, they transform the core competencies portfolio, they look for major society trends, they engage with societal needs and get inspiration for new growth areas. They invest more than average in R&D and are able to orchestrate their R&D efforts in business groups, emerging business areas, open campuses, and incubator and venture models. They are at the forefront of changing the rules of the market, instead of being surprised by market changes. They organize cross-linkages inside and outside organizational borders. These companies incorporate the ability of "lateral organizational competencies."

Figure 1 provides the key management drivers of the knowledge enterprise:

- Transformation of the business model: the deep understanding of value creation and the roadmap of firms who have been reinventing their knowledge ambition and business models in a fundamental way.
- Engagement to meet unmet customer needs.
- Address the sustainability challenges and societal demands.
- Orchestration for new business to ensure the proper flow of knowledge and R&D investments through the corporate structure. The formation of lateral linkages is a crucial instrument in the development of new competencies.

Fig. 1. Management drivers of the knowledge enterprise.

- Lateral organization in order to engender an enabling organizational structure to leverage the innovation efforts, explore new and emerging business areas, encourage entrepreneurial venturing and at the same time exploit core competencies.

However, is it not true that knowledge has always been a self-evident factor in company strategy? Of course, knowledge is a self-evident factor in many firms. It is for that very reason that the business community has invested more and more in knowledge development.

But a company's struggle might center on what valuable knowledge the firm actually possesses, and whether or not this knowledge is vitally important for the firm's competitive advantage today and tomorrow. It raises the question as to whether the current business model is protected against the law of value erosion. Some domains of knowledge can be a cash cow and should be exploited while some only have a temporary cash-generating capacity. The strategic process of companies to address the knowledge ambition and the corporate mission is the quest for "doing the right things (right)" and the corporate mission and company credo of "knowing the right direction." Often simple product innovations and simple strategic adaptations to market conditions are not enough anymore, and the firm has no other option than to reframe itself. Some companies have taken the time for deep strategic change and finding the next core business. Chapter 2 gives an overview of the quest for new business models and addresses the transformation cycle for value creation and innovation.

Chapters 3–5 elaborate on insightful and intriguing perspectives from the business cases. They address the actual transformations made of management practices of the European enterprises. These chapters present the company case studies, which serve to illustrate the development of the knowledge enterprise of European and worldwide market leaders and international network organizations. These are diverse enterprises working in the services sector, pharmaceutical sector, chemical sector, industry sector, food sector, and life sciences sector. We present the major business cases of:

- Royal DSM.
- Janssen Pharmaceutical companies of Johnson & Johnson.
- Newtricious.
- High Tech Campus Eindhoven.

The cases include longitudinal case study research made of the companies (den Hertog & Huizenga, 2000; Huizenga, 2004; Yin, 1989). We delved into the recent management practices of (inter)national firms operating in the global markets which have expanded their market borders and entered new emerging market areas. We present good practices, although it is not the intention to present best practices cases. Real changes and transformations cannot take place by merely copying best practices. Organizational innovation is predominantly a learning process that requires inspiration, insight, evidence from consistent management and recognition.

The lateral organization

Several strategies (see Chapter 6) seem effective to design for value and knowledge creation. The better performing companies have the ability to organize the synergy between knowledge and functions. The design of lateral organization structures is described. This requires the creation of new connections within the organization and connections towards customers, other enterprises, societal stakeholders and knowledge institutions. The answer will not be found in organizing in a traditional matter. Organizing by means of bureaucracy (functional domains, hierarchy, strict rules and protocols for sales, operations, production, marketing), hedging R&D and an internal focus on streamlining is the wrong direction. Management is aware of the disadvantages of such a direction and organizations have learned from past experiences.

The organizational question arising is what else can help to transform in the right direction? And what can be described as the "right direction?" Organizations should aim their cross hairs on what is happening outside of their sector because the outer world of the society and customer is more or less like a living lab. In this context the keys are learning from external developments and absorbing this know-how into the organization, and being capable of truly understanding the dynamics of the outside world. It is also notable that new forms of steering and responsibility, those that go beyond the borders of marketing, technology and R&D, can improve innovation. The design of the organization asks for new guidelines on, for example, the openness of the R&D activities, the level of co-creation with external partners and investing and organizing the critical role of new business growth. The lateral organization, in other words the capability of crossing organizational borders, is a starting point. Ultimately, these cases and practices from the companies show the ability of lateral thinking in these organizations. In this chapter we take a look at the transition process that firms have gone through when realizing their strategic ambitions. Lateral organization is a management concept and a "way of thinking and a way of acting." It is the ability of the enterprise to reach beyond the boundaries of one's own organizational domain and manage cross-functional linkages.

Business innovation — customer centricity and collaboration are key

Innovation is a complex and risky process. The pressures are high. As product life cycles are tending to become shorter and shorter, time-to-market has become crucial. Investors want to see their returns fast. For decades managers and professionals have been looking for tools and models to plan their innovative action and control the risks. One might regard the company efforts of the past five to ten years as an internal re-engineering and streamlining of the innovation process.

The struggle in Europe, Asia and the US is no longer about cost-cutting, streamlining processes, producing quality and price competition. They still remain the market entry conditions under which existing products and services can be sold. In other words, they are the defensive weapons used to protect a firm's market share. The use of defensive weapons is becoming increasingly difficult for companies. Due to high knowledge intensity and craftsmanship in all global regions, like the Middle East, Asia and other fast-growing economies, ground must be conceded continuously. Thus, factories move to other producing regions; customer services are operated from Turkey or India.

Competitive advantage and growth require other, unique competencies. The weapon of attack is the added value that other firms and institutions cannot deliver. In Europe, such added value will come from exclusive knowledge in the future, knowledge of emerging business areas and knowledge developed in collaboration with value chain partners. This will happen in knowledge and market areas that are scouted early, continuously in motion and difficult to imitate. Hence, innovation of goods, services and processes will become the key source of differentiation for Western firms (den Hertog, 2000). There are several ways to build up such competencies:

- The integration of products and services.
- The shift from bulk products (and services) to specialties.
- The development of unique process knowledge.
- Renewed interest in radical innovation.
- Dwell into the unmet customer needs and customer experiences.
- Adapting the prevailing business model to the major societal trends on energy, health and aging population.

But we observe a shift in thinking and practices. Chapter 7 considers the organization of knowledge and accompanying collaboration styles. The management practice in the 1990s focussed for a long time on the key success factors of new product and process development (Cooper, 1999; Huizenga, 2004). Internal cooperation was one of the key success factors. In the literature, the relevance of services innovation has grown, pointing out the intangible values from services and service aspects of products (Chesbrough, 2011; Ettlie & Rosenthal, 2011; Huizenga, 2004; Nijssen *et al.*, 2006; Shankar *et al.*, 2009; Tidd, 2004). More recently customer experience as an innovation and value driver gained management attention from McKinsey consultants Rawson, Duncan and Jones (2013). The prediction is that in the coming years the tendency to "think for the customer" will change radically as a result of the revolutionary developments in the field of measurability of customer experiences and (sub)conscious perceptions. The prevailing model of "inside–out" will disappear for an "outside–in" model, and consequently companies will be more and more able to map the unmet customer needs. To understand these needs requires determining customer subconscious motivations. In this respect companies need to learn to dive into the subconscious of the customers (Zaltman, 2003). It will be increasingly apparent that firms who integrate these unmet, subconscious needs into new generations of products and service will be more successful. We are witnessing the emergence of customer journeys, lab environments like living labs (Almiral & Wareham, 2011), and experience labs, in which the emotional context of customer preferences and customer behavior is accurately studied.

The other major shift in thinking and practices is with open innovation. Open innovation is the emerging dominant trend over the past few years (Chesborough, 2006). Companies have a strong tendency to think in terms of good practices and learning-by-doing. Practices are recorded on the organization of open innovation, and open innovations seems to be beyond the management hype and actually record measurable successes. When looking at the company horizon of successive transformations of DSM, Janssen Pharmaceutical companies of Johnson & Johnson, Newtricious and High Tech Campus Eindhoven, the collaboration modus of organizations is a driving force for innovation. Collaboration lies at the heart of these firms and they have succeeded in taking strong actions. They have transformed their R&D models. In addition they have built up a knowledge system, processes and organizational dynamics and a working routine in the organization to meet the customer needs, tackle sustainability challenges and build a viable route for growth. These firms teach us that collaboration takes many forms. Some firms orchestrate their thinking capacity in R&D clusters. Other companies provide strategic lateral linkages across business units, like technology councils. These forms particularly address the inflow and outflow of knowledge in R&D. These knowledge flows are directly linked to either global developments, new technology domains outside the company or to emerging business areas. We will delve into the practices and the dynamics of these forms of collaboration and the accompanying organizational design.

What can senior leaders do to stretch the depth and scope of their companies' businesses? How can they initiate major transformations proactively? The company stories will teach us that enduring commitment is a prerequisite and applying standard recipes to corporate transformations is ineffective. There is no one best-in-class approach, but what is needed is a new perspective and approach that enables executives to transform organizations proactively. The company stories each reveal their own approach and the lessons that can be learned from industry leaders.

These companies teach us, and are convinced themselves, that in the coming years company growth and competitive advantage will be determined by the firm's ability to deal with engagement and collaboration.

Chapter 2

The Knowledge Ambition — Roadmap for Value Creation

Why is the Knowledge Factor Important Right Now?

Is it not true that knowledge has always been a self-evident factor in company strategy? Of course, it is in many firms. It is for that very reason that the business community invests more and more in knowledge development. Gross domestic expenditures on research and development (R&D) stood at €245,673 million in the EU (Eurostat, 2013) in 2010, which was a 3.8% increase on the year before, and some 43.5% higher than ten years earlier (in 2000). It's for that very reason that large companies such as Philips, Shell and Unilever have protected their prestigious R&D laboratories for such a long time, and national governments underline the importance of innovation and an open knowledge infrastructure. In northwestern Europe (as defined by the European Commission), more money is spent on fundamental research than in Japan. It is for that same reason that the average company has maintained its large R&D capacity for so long. Knowledge has long been a self-evident factor, although one that nobody was talking about it. However, there are clear reasons why the knowledge factor is given priority on the strategy agenda of firms and institutions.

The Knowledge Ambition

What knowledge does a firm possess? What knowledge is vitally important for a firm's competitive advantage today and tomorrow? Which domains of knowledge should be better exploited or only have a temporary cash-generating capacity? In which fields of knowledge do firms want to catch up, or take a lead? Each of these questions is relevant to the knowledge enterprise. These questions are concerned with the roots of the company and the strategic directions taken by the company for the future. "What are we good at and passionate about, and how can we become the best in the world at those things?" The answer to this quandry is the knowledge ambition: "Doing the right things right in the quest for new value." In this quest for new value the business landscape is transforming itself constantly. Innovations and new strategies are often not enough anymore, and the firm has no other option than to reframe itself. It is the time for deep strategic change and finding the next core business. It is also about a story of new value that is still unfolding . . .

The value erosion is accelerated by the rapid pace of new technologies. Technology still makes giant leaps forward in changing the business processes and the customer processes. New phenomena appear, for example the role of services, customer experience and customer engagement. This is changing the business models of many companies:

- Pharmaceutical companies do not provide patented medicines anymore but aim at streamlining care cycles.
- Technical companies have transformed to become solution providers for engineering.

- ICT companies have appeared, which facilitates the process of social networks.
- Chemical companies have started supporting local neighborhoods, helping to fight poverty and painting housing communities in Brazil.
- Retail stores have vanished, replaced by online shopping or have become shopping experiences and megastores.
- Companies in fashion and multimedia industries have become beloved brands with profitable online business models.

When defining the knowledge ambition of the organization, competencies will be defined and assessed. What are the current competencies? How important are these for the organization? What is their relevance in the future? What are the core competencies that distinguish the firm from others? Which are the firm's enabling competencies, essential in order to create added value, and which ones are imitable or exchangeable? The ambition of the knowledge enterprise is underscored by this focus on creating value. New value is created by innovation in products, markets and processes. In this context, the continuous search for new sources of value is a basic remedy for value erosion, and innovation of products and services is one of the main routes towards the creation of new value. In the 1980s, innovation used to look like a scientific laboratory or a makeshift center for engineering new products and processes in the backyard. Then, talking about innovation was talking about technology push and market pull.

Since then, our views on innovation have changed. We are becoming aware that product or service innovation are not the only sources of generating new value. Value can be generated along the whole internal and external value chain, even along foreign value chains. Firms have to develop the capability to find out how (Sawhney & Parikh, 2001) economic value behaves. They have to go and find it at the margin of the value chains and networks, those closest to the customer. They have to go where new consumer needs are emerging (Eyring *et al.*, 2011). They need to look for value in combining a product with a service, or vice versa, or identifying emerging markets and customer segments to improve their bottom and top lines.

Innovation nowadays is about strengthening the existing R&D competencies and a sustained dedication to developing new competencies. This has to be done in order to tap into opportunities in (emerging) fast-growing markets and pioneer value segments around the globe. Companies must learn the customer developments, trends and business rules in countries in Asia, the Pacific, Latin America and Africa.

The arrival of the online channel has taught us that innovation is to be anchored in customer value. In this perspective, innovation becomes a continuous quest for better business: business innovation. Adequate understanding of value creation becomes a must and firms have thus been reinventing their *knowledge ambition* and *business models* in a fundamental way (Johnson *et al.*, 2009; Volberda *et al.*, 2013).

Chapters 3–5 of this book examine in detail the business transformations of international companies in order to manage innovation in a range of businesses. Each case is accompanied by the leading questions on transforming the organization. They reveal on the one hand the knowledge ambitions of the company and on the other hand the roadmap for the pursuit of value creation.

In one example, the historical roots of a company have been set aside and the firm has developed the ambition to create a better life for people. The ambition is clear. But how should core competencies be redesigned and how should strategic choices be made on innovation and R&D to ensure consistent growth? A similar desire can be noted as driving the development of companies' open campus models. The ambition, again, is clear: to create innovation hotspots; to bring together competencies that enable new business; to collect state-of-the-art competencies and firms and become and remain the "smartest region of the world." The transition towards this accompanying business model raises several challenges. How can the ecosystem for open innovation flourish in the high-tech sector? How is it possible to create a powerful R&D cluster, become one of the largest science parks in the world and design a successful model for open innovation? Similarly, the pharmaceutical sector is an industry facing several major challenges. The ambition of being able to solve patients' unmet medical needs has led to promising results. This requires a transformation in order to identify the new sources of value. How does a company transform its knowledge organization in search of breakthroughs in healthcare-related competencies? A remarkable example is the reframing of the core business of agriculture towards food nutrition and healthcare. The ambition of discovering the ultimate value of agricultural products requires an understanding of new knowledge domains in the life sciences segment. How can a European market leader in the production and distribution of agricultural products, transform into a knowledge enterprise in the food nutrition and life sciences sector? In the roadmap of collaboration and co-creation we encounter the practices of multinationals on their corporate research efforts in discovering a new business model of open innovation. How can co-creation become a viable business model and be valuable to both large corporations and start-up high-tech ventures?

"Knowing the right things" is the slogan when the direction must be determined and choices need to be made. This sounds logical, but "knowing" and "knowledge" are abstract notions.

The Corporate Mission Defines the Knowledge Ambition

The notion of the knowledge enterprise presupposes that we are able to determine what "knowledge" is, which pieces of knowledge to explore and which ones to exploit. Different types of knowledge can be named and given characteristics. "Functional knowledge," that is knowledge that is developed within disciplines or business areas, appears in domains like life sciences, material sciences and food sciences. "Operational knowledge" is based upon operational processes and embedded in procedures and control mechanisms. "Contextual knowledge" refers to an understanding of the surroundings of the organization, and a deep understanding of customers. Knowledge about the context (society, sustainability, technology, etc.) within which the firm operates is also indispensable.

The knowledge development process itself in, for example, R&D and seizing new growth opportunities and core competencies, is also a field of corporate discussion. The systems view of organizational learning is especially helpful here. The business community is convinced that the underlying notion is that there is a constant change of the knowledge needed by the organization. Apart from continuous change of the product, service or accompanying process or technology, constant movement (i.e. a change of place) is another essential characteristic of knowledge. Knowledge flows from one development department, or organizational unit, to the other, from developers to users, from unit to unit, from emerging business area to the existing market divisions, from outside to inside the organization, back and forth.

An often used, and comprehensive, distinction, is to divide knowledge into explicit and tacit (or implicit) knowledge. Tacit knowledge is not written down, but built up and stored in the employees' brains. This particular type of knowledge is a source of constant attention from organizations. Tacit knowledge is also embedded in the culture of an organization. It is, moreover, a vehicle for creativity and innovation, as well as a limit on change ("not-invented-here"). Core competencies turn into incompetence when holding on to obsolete implicit knowledge. The knowledge enterprise is an organization perspective that claims that corporations which only steer based on explicit knowledge are heading for destruction (Drucker, 1998).

Firms have to understand several types of knowledge, such as unaddressed customer needs, and innovate to create new value and to safeguard their future. One clue to this puzzle is the corporate strategy and knowledge ambition, which is more important than ever. It is about gaining market share and creating mindshare with customers. In our highly competitive world, this is becoming more complex as most markets are changing fast. With the technology radically changing traditional marketing disciplines, the challenge is to successfully merge new and old competencies. Formulating the knowledge ambition implies that choices are made between competencies. It is thus possible to determine the strategic importance of different competencies. For that purpose, later in this chapter the distinction between core competencies, enabling competencies and exchangeable competencies is introduced.

The starting point for the knowledge enterprise is the definition of the knowledge ambition, which often reflects the corporate identity and future direction for growth. Over the decades the firms have been guided by its corporate mission, strategic foresight on its core business and a transformation of its knowledge structure. This ability to change is a typical company characteristic and seems to be grounded in the roots of the company by means of:

- Strategic foresight and purpose.
- A strategic focus to understand and respond to global society trends.
- An enduring commitment to stretching its core competencies.
- An innovation climate: an innovation-based culture and advocacy for (scientific) breakthroughs.
- A supporting governance structure for the knowledge and knowledge flows in the organization.

When defining the knowledge ambition several aspects are of importance in order to ensure that the corporate mission is accepted, shared, committed to and clearly communicated both internally and externally. Among these are the following dimensions:

1. **The process in defining the ambition**: the iterative and good-to-great approach are two different ways of defining the company's direction and the subsequent consequences on the knowledge and competencies that the company should focus on.
2. **The ambition and corporate mission as a guide for the competency direction**: the purpose, the mission, the credo, the empowerment of people and the impact on the portfolio of competencies.
3. **The deep dives and the strategic dialogues at senior management level**: this includes, amongst other things, defining the change-forcing objectives, the buy in from

senior management, the leadership style and management capabilities.

4. **Which competencies belong to the core?**: the exploration and exploitation of competencies, the division of current and emerging competencies and the accompanying investments and divestments.

The Process in Defining the Ambition: The Sequential and Good-to-Great Approaches

When formulating strategic plans, we are used to placing the activities needed for them in a fixed, logical order. They are often embedded in a long-range and annual-operating plan. The construction of this planning is a sequential, structured process, and commonly falls in line with a yearly or quarterly budget and planning cycle. First, the environment is explored, which serves as a self-inspection. On the basis of the developments in the environment possible scenarios are then formulated. These scenarios are compared to the internal state of affairs, thus indicating "gaps" between what is desired and what is available in reality. The gap analysis leads to the choice of the most suitable scenario and the definition of change objectives. In this sequential approach, tasks are usually split up into sub-tasks, which are subsequently divided into the existing parts of the organization, e.g. plans and targets for the business (units, lines, departments). In this "sequential approach" the knowledge ambition and the core competencies are a derivative of the firm's strategic planning process.

On the other hand a corporation can define the ambition in line with the classic good-to-great (Collins, 2001) or great-by-choice (Collins & Hansen, 2011) philosophies. Ten years after the worldwide bestseller *Good to Great*, Collins and Hansen ask (Collins & Hansen, 2011) why some companies thrive in times of uncertainty and others companies do not. Based on nine years of research, Collins and Hansen set out the principles for building a great enterprise in unpredictable, tumultuous and hectic times.

The basic management message of this work is that companies who want to go from good to great need to transcend this simplistic way of thinking about competencies. Good is the enemy of great and competencies can direct a company's transformation into a mediocre position if it does not generate value or differentiate. Why? First, the good-to-great companies founded their strategies on deep understanding along three key dimensions: be the best, be passionate and keep a well-oiled economic engine. These good-to-great companies also focussed on "what not to do" and what they should stop doing (divest, spinout ventures etc.). Second, the good-to-great companies translated that understanding into a simple, bright concept (e.g. knowledge ambition) that guided all their efforts, described as the hedgehog concept and change-forcing objectives. More precisely, a hedgehog concept is a simple, clear concept that flows from deep understanding about the intersection of three strategic themes (Fig. 1).

1. *What you can be the best in the world at* (and, equally important, what you cannot be the best in the world at). This question goes beyond the current core competency. Just because you possess a core competency doesn't necessarily mean you can be the best in the world at it. Conversely, what you can be the best at might not even be something in which you are currently engaged. So the key driver is what the corporation's vision of the future is about.

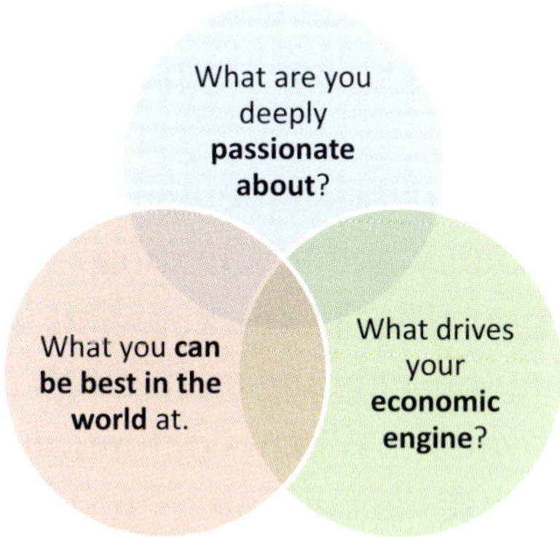

Fig. 1. Three circles forming the hedgehog concept (source: Collins, 2001). Copyright © 2001. Reprinted by permission of Curtis Brown, Ltd.

2. *Question the current business model on the economic logic and the economic engine.* In this philosophy corporations obtain clear, fact-based insights into the economic drivers; more precisely, the drivers that generate sustained and robust cash flow and profitability.
3. *What is the corporation deeply passionate about?* Collins (2001; see also Collins & Hansen, 2011) observed that the good-to-great companies focussed on those activities that spark and fire their passion. The idea here is not to stimulate passion but to discover what you are actually passionate about.

When defining the knowledge ambition, the use of a sequential approach is strongly advised against for two important reasons. Firstly, in doing so, the knowledge ambition is understood as a derivative of the strategic objective of the firm. Yet, competencies, and core competencies in particular, are at the same time the breeding ground for the firm's strategic positioning. What the firm *can* do determines to a great extent its opportunities in transformational and adjacent innovations. This means that the approach will have to possess a strongly iterative character.

A second objection to the sequential approach is that it leads to hedging of technology and to situations of segmentation and compartmentalization. That is, the knowledge becomes hedged in separate units, namely existing technology domains, which is ineffective for innovation. When a definition of the knowledge ambition breaks up tasks according to the existing organization and technology portfolio, it is very likely that the firm does not make any progress whatsoever. There is a risk that existing technology departments and other projects or units of the firm will try to retain their own knowledge domains, with the consequent chance of sub-optimization or them even becoming obsolete. Attempts to connect these with one another usually result in patchwork, stuck-in-the-middle and stabilizing market positions.

One might view the business strategy (see Fig. 2) as a multiplier which can be used to "stretch" the current competencies and the knowledge ambition. The current and desired competencies are linked to one another, metaphorically speaking, by an elastic band. The business strategy can reach further as the distance between current and desired competencies is stretched. However, it takes an effort to stretch the current competencies

Fig. 2. Business strategy as a multiplier for future competencies.

to engender the desired competencies. The power exerted to achieve this is dependent on the urgency, corporate passion and scope of the new business strategy. It should also be noted that companies with a strong heritage, long-lasting history or a broad family of companies are often committed to keeping their mission and passion going, unless economic logic advises otherwise.

Race cycling technology or creating a better cycling experience

The above-described route explains the dynamic link between market pull and technology push. An example from the sports sector will illustrate this. Race cycling manufactures such as Giant, Bianchi, Koga Miyata, Orbea and Cervélo have long since focussed on the perfection of cycling frames. Over the past decade in many cycling events the uphill climb stage and speed records have been broken, partially due to the introduction of new materials and technological breakthroughs, for example lightweight race frames. The famous mountain climbs (Mont Ventoux and Alpe d'Huez in France, Stelvio in Italy) have witnessed new time records. Over the years, special bikes have been developed with improved aerodynamics, frames and air-tight wheels, and the use of increasingly sophisticated aerodynamics has continued. Let us take as an example one of these companies and let us presume their mission and passion is to create a better cycling experience for people around the world. The spirit of sport is the common value shared by the employees. Engineering is not at the core of what they do, people's cycling experiences is the key driver of what the corporation's vision of the future is about.

In this example case the company has to make the strategic choice to develop products with a higher added value. Two new market segments are being considered as being part of this strategy:

- The high growth market for mountain bikes.
- The market for aerodynamic monocoque carbon cycle frames.

When looking at the firm's current know-how, the first option appears to be too ambitious. It requires building up a new competency in this market area and learning how to understand customer experiences. The firm lacks the know-how about the mountain bike market, entry conditions, product proficiency, distribution network, and knowledge of the sport's customer insights. The second option seems feasible, because the firm had previously gained experience with the design and manufacturing of frames in different sizes and in terms of product composition. The firm possesses the technological know-how, employs R&D staff and the product can be developed in collaboration with carbon technology specialists. Additionally, it does not seem to be too difficult to recruit technical engineers in this field. But, choosing the first option is persuasive as it fits with the corporate passion and strategic foresight. This leads to the question within the firm as to whether pursuit of the mountain bike segment is a "blue ocean strategy" that could be extended to include a broader segment, e.g. beach cruisers or hybrid city bikes. This is exemplary for a discussion of reinventing the business model into a new market (Zott and Amit, 2008). This example demonstrates that the company would initially be limited by the existing set of competencies.

The Ambition and Corporate Mission as a Guide for the Competency Direction

The knowledge ambition indicates the roots of the firm, the current position and the future direction. Even more so it can be based on the legacy of the founders or be derived from a historical tradition. A clearly defined knowledge ambition can be a driving force for the business development and above all a motivating force for employees. Ambitions take several communication expressions like, for example, the company brand promise, the pay-off or the company credo and the unwritten rules of the corporation. They can serve as the daily guidelines for all the work done by people within the company, and they give direction to the competencies a firm needs to possess in order to fulfil the brand promise.

Ritz-Carlton — redefining hotel industry

Take for example Horst Schulze, former president of the Ritz-Carlton Hotel Company, who founded the group on the basis that he was not just selling rooms and food, he was selling service (Bell, 2012). In a nutshell, the company credo is (Ritz-Carlton, 2014):

> . . . the Ritz-Carlton Hotel is a place where the genuine care and comfort of the guests is the highest mission. They pledge to provide the finest personal service and facilities for guests who will always enjoy a warm, relaxed yet refined atmosphere. The Ritz-Carlton experience enlivens the senses, instils well-being, and fulfils even the unexpressed wishes and needs of guests . . .

The Ritz-Carlton has become a unique brand. Schulze wanted guests to feel that they did not want to go home. There are now Ritz-Carlton hotels all over the world, and their mission is clear: The Ritz-Carlton Hotel Company must be regarded as the quality leader of the hotel industry worldwide. This has been packaged in the "Ritz-Carlton service values," which are an expression of this ambition. Here, the Ritz-Carlton defined a credo of 20 service statements that guide their employees in servicing customers. In daily operations employees perform "daily quality line-up meetings" to assess their own service practices and routines. The credo will be known, appropriated and energized by all employees. The company motto is crystal clear: "We are Ladies and Gentlemen serving Ladies and Gentlemen." Among their service values are other guidelines such as:

- Practice team work and "lateral service" to create a positive work environment.
- All employees will successfully complete training certification to ensure they understand how to perform to the Ritz-Carlton standards in their position.

Often, such companies operate through a unique culture that values and fosters the development of its people. Horst Schultz is now redefining the hotel industry once again with Capella Hotel Group and defining the new frontier in luxury: ultra-luxury.

Accordingly, the knowledge ambition directs the people working in the organization. At the same it gives direction to the organizational needs (or even requirements) of the competencies portfolio. Direction is given and decisions should be taken on:

- The competencies the organization possesses.
- The relevance of the current competencies to the firm.
- The competencies the firm must (further) develop in order to achieve the strategic objectives.
- The competencies that can be cut back, set aside, allocated in a joint venture or sold off.

The knowledge ambition is at the basis for determining the demands that should be placed on the organization of the knowledge enterprise.

In making the ambitions explicit and communicable the knowledge ambition is formulated in credo statements, in annual reports and communication documents, which should be clear and transparent to all those involved. The document is formulated for different target groups to empower them in their daily work. It's a guide for (senior) management and staff responsible for achieving the ambition. It's a statement to clients that are engaged with the firm on the basis of its products, services and competencies (in particular when considering business-to-business relationships). It is also a guide for external ventures, enterprises and investors that are looking for collaboration or in financing competencies for their portfolio.

It is obvious that the form of the knowledge ambition can vary in detail, depending on the audience. A good indicator for the quality of the ambition is the degree to which it is explicitly stated in corporate communications (website to investment reports), shared and consistently used as a navigator for the company transformation. The knowledge ambition gives sense of direction; in other words the challenge or the stretch of the current business model.

Deep Dives and Strategic Dialogues

The ambition is an instrument to move the organization in the desired direction. A transformational function to help the company journey move in the right direction. Collins (2001; see also Collins & Hansen, 2011) talks about a "make it happen culture of discipline" and later the "20-Mile March." The motivation behind this culture is that discipline combined with the ethics of entrepreneurship will create better (great) results. The 20-Mile March is an approach to have concrete, clear, intelligent and rigorously pursued performance mechanisms that keep the company on track. In this point of view the company creates two zones of discomfort. First of all is the discomfort of unwavering commitment to high performance in difficult conditions, for example in pharmaceuticals and fine chemicals with fast-paced technological developments. Secondly comes the discomfort of holding back in good conditions, e.g. investments in emerging business areas and new ventures that ride good economic tides.

One precondition is that the right people are situated in the right place ("do what you are best at"). One might presume that a lot of attention should be paid to change management programs or motivational culture programs. On the contrary, as Collins (2011) already argued, we observed with the companies featured in this book that the transformation was autonomous, high-performance driven and not initiated or launched by such programs.

On the one hand this puts clear demands upon the quality of the knowledge ambition: is it challenging, inspiring or even change forcing? But this kind of quality is not sufficient. *Broad* support and employee commitment across the organization is needed to lead to concrete behavioral change. Bringing together the right expertise in a small think-tank is not enough. A diversity of ideas must be tapped, which is expected to lead to a clear focus eventually. The established interests of groups and individuals will come up for discussion, while the basis and consensus are preconditions for success. In other words: decrees from the top are equally useless as endless rounds of participation. The strategic dialogues (Senge, 1990; Stacey, 1996) are therefore an appropriate form of involvement for the development of the knowledge ambition. Stacey commented that the dialogue is a platform to exchange views about paradoxical situations, each having the intention of modifying their position before the views and evidence presented by the other. Openness is key in these dialogues, and the deep dive is an appropriate method for this. It is a combination of mind mapping, scenario prototyping and feedback loops merged into an approach that (senior) executives and teams will help to develop solutions for specific business challenges or create commitment. It is not sufficient that conflicts and hidden agendas are put on the table, and arguments and debates do not imply an intention to change. The *dialogue* is a type of communication in which this intention is inherent.

This kind of communication dialogue helps groups, units and teams in several aspects:

- To define and share the common goal.
- To understand and commit to the change forcing objectives.
- To accept the contrast in opinions and interests.
- To identify the required knowledge to get things done.
- To install 360 degrees closed-loop feedback and open communication.
- To cross organizational linkages need to pass traditional lines of hierarchy and power.

In a large organization, one can consider dialogues as among and between several management echelons and company levels.

- Strategic dialogues at senior management level. The senior leaders, who express leadership skills based on open dialogue and define the corporate mission and knowledge ambitions.
- Dialogues at division level and R&D level. The R&D and innovation management teams and councils, which indicate

the frameworks and take the final decisions on R&D investments, scientific collaborations (e.g. universities).

- The team level. The highly qualified knowledge workers and employees, those involved in the inner circle of the organization. These are also the employees from different business units, corporate and decentralized R&D, functional departments and management echelons that are part of the transformation.
- The ecosystem level. The outer circle of stakeholders, customers and suppliers in which ideas can be expressed and feedback comments are appreciated.

Building a sustainable growth path is not dependent on a single defining action, a big program, one breakthrough product, a moment of truth or incidental financial benefit. Conversely, the transformation (see Fig. 3) necessitates relentlessly pushing all parts of the corporation in the same direction, and consequently building momentum to move industry frontiers and be the first to go beyond them.

Transition leadership. During the transition years it is necessary to rely upon senior leadership: a member of the management team must continuously safeguard the translation to the business strategy and the communication to the rest of the firm. Such roles belong to the chief executive officer, chief technology officer, chief innovation officer, amongst others, who must incorporate a blend of personal humility, passion for the credo and a professional willingness to build and be change forcing. Leadership requires a company purpose and lateral thinking. Making connections between different knowledge areas, e.g. technology domains. This thinking capacity can be ensured by e.g. setting up strategy councils and (two-yearly) scenario analyses, e.g. the technological and business-sheet scenarios.

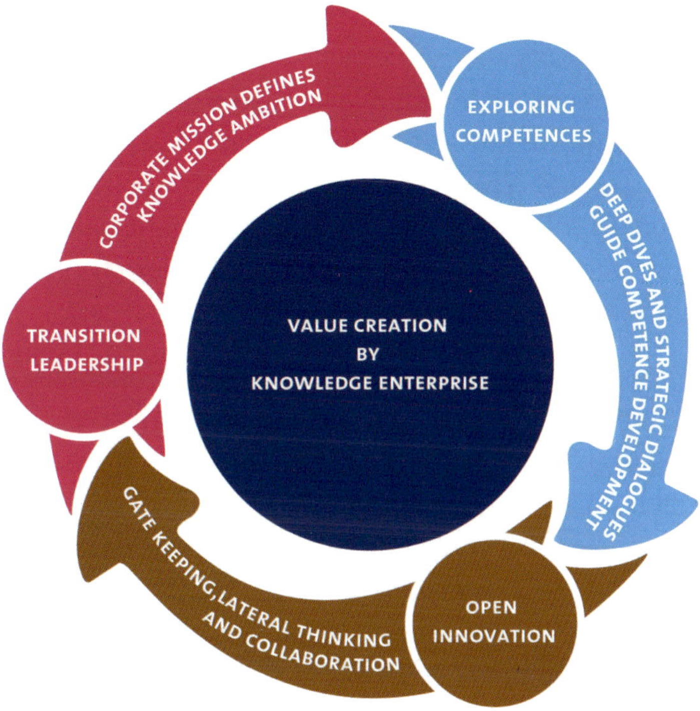

Fig. 3. Transformation circle — metamorphosis of the knowledge enterprise.

Exploring competencies. This is looking outside the organization or looking beyond one's own industry boundaries. On the one hand this involves a close interaction of corporate R&D and decentralized R&D and units dedicated to innovation (e.g. campus, innovation centers). This gate-keeping function is a crucial corporate function in safeguarding a long-term perspective of growth. Activities include scouting new technologies, combining internal knowledge and external knowledge; corporate research programs need these scouting and gate-keeping functions in order to ensure the long-term success of R&D and business opportunities. This is a critical element in the knowledge infrastructure as this role invests in the competencies, which can be either one step ahead or one step behind the current business, and business groups. This role can be organized in several ways, for example to absorb external ideas, scout new ventures or pick up external knowledge developments ("gate keeping") and market developments. This requires the room for entrepreneurship and budget to follow technological trends, start dialogues with engaged customers and look for opportunities in other value chains.

Open innovation. Especially in a situation of open innovation it is of importance to collaborate with and involve clients or external knowledge providers in this process. It assumes that firms open up for combining internal and external paths to the market, advance their technological competencies and increase competitiveness (Chesbrough, 2003). In the development of this new paradigm for innovation the managerial implications are clear:

- Create an open innovative climate.
- Concentrate on cooperation in value networks.
- Give room for (corporate) entrepreneurship.
- Provide a culture for entrepreneurship, for example with a venturing bootcamp.
- Get insights from (lead) user involvement.
- Meet the need for (regional or global) orchestration in actually sharing knowledge and venturing.

It is also an effective treatment for "not-invented-here" situations, particularly in the case of firms that are strongly internally oriented, or where certain departments possess a knowledge monopoly internally.

The final dimension involves the division of current and emerging competencies and the accompanying investments and divestments in competencies. Below we introduce the distinction between core competencies, enabling competencies and exchangeable competencies.

Which Competencies Belong to the Core

In recent years, the competencies approach has been followed by numerous firms throughout Europe, the US and Asia. Firms have learned that some business areas are more important to the organization than others. Consequently, some business-related knowledge areas (or "competencies") provide the foundation of the firm's existence. They are the engine of the business model and are the source for the development of new products, services and processes. These areas are the unique or core competencies that distinguish the firm from other firms (Hamel & Prahalad, 1994). Core competencies alone, however, do not suffice for a firm to function, and other competencies with a less unique character are needed to bring products and services into the market. Thus, a company that distinguishes from other firms on the basis of its advanced design should also possess a sound administrative system as well as a strong sales function. We call these enabling competencies (Leonard-Barton, 1995): the competencies that a firm should possess in order to operate effectively and create added value. Finally, there are competencies that can be exchanged among companies ("outsourced") fairly easily, without losing much added value or strongly affecting the firm's competitiveness.

Core competencies

Core competencies enable the firm to create markets. Within highly developed economies, it is no longer possible for firms to be competitive by doing things better, quicker and cheaper.

Serving existing markets does not suffice for firms that take their market leadership seriously. In the future, competitive advantage will be possible only by doing things that others cannot do. Consequently, firms should base their strategy on the unique knowledge and skills they possess. Within the firm, the powers must be bundled to develop these core competencies in such a way that they cannot be imitated or copied.

This management message has been successfully disseminated in these firms over the past ten years. Firms must seek the core of their abilities and determine what is needed to take and keep a decisive lead. Core competencies are identified by subjecting the most important competencies of an organization to the following criteria. Competencies belong to the core of a firm if:

- A core competency enables an organization to provide its customers with a real added value.
- A core competency provides the firm with a unique competitive advantage.
- A core competency is the basis for new business development throughout the entire organization, if they create new products and new markets.

Core competencies typically "span" business and product boundaries in the firm. Furthermore, core competencies have a dominance over products in that they evolve more slowly than the products they generate. Core competencies arise through "collective learning" and are enhanced through sharing and using knowledge. Core competencies are also strategic. Nowadays managers are aware of the strategic importance of the knowledge available within the organization and are aware of the need to make choices for the investments in R&D that really matter in the future.

Enabling and exchangeable competencies

Core competencies are the building blocks of the current business results, but also the roadmap for future success. Enabling competencies (Leonard-Barton, 1995) strongly determine the success of the company today. They make it happen in the organization. They are usually connected to the most important stages in the value chain (Porter, 1985), such as marketing, R&D and operations. Any firms can possess these competencies. In that sense, they are irreplaceable, but not unique. Enabling competencies do not distinguish a firm from others, but provide the necessary conditions to enter the market and create added value. Thus, a chemical company cannot do without knowledge of materials chemistry processing, nor can a food factory manage without a thorough knowledge of quality control.

The second characteristic of these competencies is that they are often closely entwined with the firm's core competencies. This is a result of the continuous exchange of (usually tacit) knowledge needed to bring products and services into the market that yield a profit. The product development department will involve the production department in a chemical firm in its projects at an early stage in order to anticipate processing problems or up-scaling problems. A hospital, conducting cancer surgery as a core competency, is almost unthinkable without an enabling, advanced cancer treatment and nursing department. Sometimes the enabling competencies are fully matched with the core competencies, e.g. in start-ups or early innovator ventures. For example, pure R&D ventures (firms having only R&D and, hence, pure core competency) are found in areas like life sciences, materials sciences, high-tech and pharmacy, where patents and licenses can be protected and traded. Consequently, in these firms the enabling competencies resemble the core competencies and they cannot be exchanged or split up.

Another category of competencies is the exchangeable competency. This is the sum of the know-how that can be outsourced to other organizations without it having direct consequences for the rest of the organization. This may be knowledge that can be replaced by other knowledge without crucial consequences. The most straightforward examples of exchangeable knowledge are concerned with such activities as security, pay rolling and salary administration. The boundaries between enabling and exchangeable competencies, however, differ per firm. For example, a number of pharmaceutical firms keep the chemical plants for strategic reasons inside the firm, whereas in others the assembly of active substances and additives (the "pills plant") are subcontracted.

When formulating the knowledge ambition, competencies are identified and assessed. They describe the company focus and priority, and they provide insight into the possibility of exploiting competencies effectively into profitable business.

In some organizations, the identification of core competencies does not lead to many problems, because these can be described in accepted and explicit terms (for example in chronic disease areas or science domains). But which adjacent or new competencies are relevant? When competencies are closely intertwined, it is much harder to categorize and assess these desired competencies.

The assessment of competencies is primarily a matter of reaching a consensus. This is based on a large range factors, such as:

- The risk/return ratio.
- The novelty of the knowledge for the firm and the sector.
- The success rate in the market.
- The expected business volume in the emerging business area.

- The ability to get a sustainable lead in the new market.
- The cost/benefit ratio.
- The possibility to protect intellectual property and patenting.
- The time-to-market.

The classical AD Little portfolio approach (Roussel *et al.*, 1991), which is used as the third R&D generation model in industrial and engineering firms, is helpful. This approach chooses the portfolio of R&D projects, or high-quality client projects as starting points, which are based upon risk, reward and carriers of knowledge. Systematic comparison of these projects gradually leads to an image of the firm's own competencies. Venturing and innovation centers play a crucial role in this respect.

In most cases, however, what is needed is not a fundamental and direct change of the core competencies, but gradual expansion. The knowledge ambition briefly states the most important direction for achieving this objective. The venture, bootcamp and campus models are useful mechanisms. These provide the platform for new development projects that fit in with the firm's ambition and may or may not be implemented in cooperation with other firms and which may ultimately serve to make the new business lines more visible.

Exploring competencies

The decision to retain a competency inside the firm and label it as "enabling" is made in practice on the basis of several arguments and criteria: the competency does not generate the expected business results (over a couple of years); the competency is no longer crucial for the business growth path and future portfolio (e.g. sell the competency); the firm can outsource or stop the competency, because other firms can do it better and cheaper, e.g. in the flat-screen TV business; or the competency is becoming obsolete and has lost "competition-sensitive" know-how.

The decision to acquire or build up new competencies is not an easy job. The knowledge system of firms thrives on bringing people together, exchanging people and ideas, and exploiting competencies. When competencies are primarily applied by one business unit or group, it is the senior managers' responsibility to share these competencies with other business groups. At the same time it is a delicate journey to identify the missing competencies. Which new competencies should be explored and do they provide a window of opportunity? Firms make strategic acquisitions in this area. As part of their growth strategy, firms can enter into partnerships with companies or organizations possessing competencies in fields where the company intends to grow. In light of this, the venturing function of the corporations has a decisive role. Mergers and acquisitions strategy is aimed at acquiring missing competencies, for example in new medical domains, nutrition and bio-based fuels. Such partnerships are a way of pooling knowledge and resources.

Venture and entrepreneurship

In the next chapter we will explore this corporate process of venturing and scouting. Corporations have installed innovation centers with a clear new business target and/or a science discovery role. They function as the scout and gate keeper. They are equipped with resources and investment mandates to build relationships with technological start-ups, academic institutes and other stakeholders in new business domains. The innovations center's role is to discover and explore the best early-stage science in the world and to close early-stage deals.

In the high-tech, pharmaceutical and chemical domains we will see an exploratory role for the campus model. A crucial part of the campus strategy incorporates a business development hub. In this strategy, the corporate goals are directed at:

- Exploring new technological competencies.
- Stimulating promising internal and external opportunities with the potential to generate new sustainable solutions.
- Creating a venture pool, and launching projects, ventures or healthcare businesses, adjacent to the company core business.
- Fostering, deploying, and attracting scientific and entrepreneurial talent.

A precondition for achieving results (and leadership in an industry) is a large and permanent investment in new knowledge, which impacts the R&D levels and the firms' financial bases. Once cooperation in this area with other firms appears unrealistic, the firm can decide to sell the division and invest the money made in the development of the other core competencies.

These roles are of significant importance as it fosters knowledge development and guides the companies towards viable business results.

What if...

But what happens if the company's structure and R&D processes are not capable of fulfilling that knowledge ambition? What if the required capabilities for the current business are satisfactory, but transformational capabilities are not present in the organization? This results in the contrary process: less envisioning by senior management, less efforts in deeply understanding customer needs, less investments in developing emerging business and go-to-market practices. This is the classical pattern of incremental innovations, innovations close to its core business, optimizing existing products, market strategies and competencies. Core competencies become enabling competencies and eventually become obsolete. "Not-invented-here" ideas, which might be worthwhile, are put on hold, small ventures are put under pressure by time or budget constraints, or are simply ignored on the basis of the revenue figures and weight in the portfolio of the enterprise.

The Moments of Truth in the Business Economy

One might presume that the position of the knowledge enterprise in the world economic system is vulnerable. Companies are vulnerable to the drivers of value erosion and are constantly fighting the law of value erosion. As soon as goods and services exchanged in an open market are introduced to that market, they start to lose value. Imitation and the introduction of new and better alternatives are the most important drivers of this value erosion. However, institutional change and the opening of markets (transparency) can also play a major role. To counter value erosion, firms have to find other and new ways of value creation. They have to make a choice for strategies like:

- The introduction of new products and processes.
- Focus on better, higher added-value products.
- Focus on better customers, providing higher margins at lower costs.
- Adding services to products.
- Adding products to services.
- Managing value chains.
- Creation of systems of products and services.
- New ways of customer interaction.

Companies that wish to stay competitive and aim for sustainable growth face a tough economic climate, and a tough time in riding the economic waves. This is further compounded by the need to align with societal conditions, changing monetary systems, technological progress and competition.

But this perception is radically opposite to the encountered business practices. The companies which were interviewed seem dedicated, even persistent in leveraging their core competencies. They are in a constant process of adapting the strategy and the structure to meet the business demands. This is a crucial, insightful and intriguing consideration.

Business Case Study Approach

We (myself and a team of business managers) conducted case study research with international corporations and networks of companies that have transformed their business models successfully to meet new conditions in their respective industries. Chapters 3–5 present the company case studies, which serve to illustrate the development of the knowledge enterprise of European and worldwide market leaders and international network organizations. To this end we consider enterprises present in the services, pharmaceutical, chemical, industry, food, and life sciences sectors. Precisely, we present the cases of DSM, Janssen Pharmaceutical companies of Johnson & Johnson, Newtricious and High Tech Campus Eindhoven. The cases include longitudinal case study research of the companies (den Hertog & Huizenga, 2000; Huizenga 2004). We delve into the recent management practices of these international firms, which are operating in global markets and which expand their market borders and constantly enter new emerging market areas.

We present the good practices, managerial lessons learned and the company decision made over the past years, although it is not a recipe for success or presentation of best practices. Real changes and transformations cannot take place by merely copying best practices. Organizational innovation is predominantly a learning process that requires inspiration, insight, evidence from consistent management and recognition.

Ultimately, these companies show the ability to question their revenue model and the competency of lateral thinking within the organization; that is, thinking beyond the boundaries of one's own organizational domain.

We conducted semi-structured interviews lasting two hours with many executives and managers at each company. Each interview was recorded, transcribed and coded. In addition we collected documents on the companies practices and performances (e.g. investments, research and development (R&D) figures etc.) over the past five years. An in-depth case study was written about each company. Each case was reviewed by multiple stakeholders in the company for approval. In the interviews we spoke with, amongst others, the senior leaders of the corporations, e.g.:

- Chief executive officers (CEO).
- Chief technology officers (CTO).
- Chief innovation officers (CIO).
- Senior vice presidents responsible for R&D.
- Senior vice presidents responsible for campus strategy.
- Communications managers and brand managers.
- R&D managers and chief scientists.
- Managing directors of Belgium, the Netherlands and Luxembourg (Benelux) and Europe, the Middle East and Asia (EMEA).
- Business development managers.

Some important interview questions we asked concerned their perceptions and the raw facts of the organizational transformation, the business model and the value creation strategy. We asked them about the driving role of innovation and the accompanying organization (re)design. We delved deep into the lessons learned, the good practices and strategic experiments and the competencies and R&D strategies. On the interview agenda of the CEOs were the questions: how do you perceive the industry will be shaped in the next three to five years? Which trends and societal scenarios are relevant? What must be done to ensure that the company and the industry evolves in that direction? What mission can guide this transformation? What skills and competencies are needed to raise the organization towards the next level? And how does one organize the competency portfolio to broaden beyond the business boundaries?

The most prevalent pattern in all the interview data was that each of the enterprises, in a sense, reinvented their industry and showed a performance-oriented culture and a disciplined strategic planning process. Furthermore the data showed the companies' ability to regenerate their own competency strategy: knowing what the core competencies bring the corporation, assessing the competency portfolio and investing and exploring enabling and core competencies.

The company cases are based on the strategic interviews, academic research and consulting programs performed in the period 2013–2014. We also conducted longitudinal analyses of the companies over the past ten to twelve years (the period 2000–2012). Furthermore, we introduced cross-sector company cases, based on their relevant corporate story and evidence. Some of the companies (e.g. DSM) took part in the earlier longitudinal study (den Hertog & Huizenga, 2000). This case study was commissioned by the EU and performed by UNU MERIT (United Nations University, Maastricht Economic Research Institute on Innovation and Technology) (den Hertog & Huizenga 2000). Managerial insights were also compared from the large benchmark and case survey study on key success factors on innovation within the technology industry (Huizenga, 2004) and the study on innovation management in the processing industry (den Hertog *et al.*, 2000). We conducted a literature survey, included opinion articles and news reports, and held exploratory interviews with managers from a range of companies and several innovation programs. In the past years we have also conducted several consulting programs with innovation managers from companies. This all served as a preparation. In the study itself, open interviews were held with the senior leaders per company who had been involved in various roles in organizational innovation processes within their firms. Both the corporate organization and the business divisions were involved in this case study process. We got access to all sorts of company information, regarding the company strategy, innovation projects and internal communication reports.

With the emergence of the network organization and open innovation we included two cases on leading network and campus initiatives in the high-tech sector and food and pharmaceutical sector. The resulting case reports have been thoroughly discussed with the representatives of these firms. Industry-leading companies have been incorporated for this study. Some companies have been earlier described elsewhere (e.g. DSM by van Leen (2010) and den Hertog and Huizenga (2000)). For the study, we selected firms working in both the chemical, high-tech industry and the pharmaceutical and nutrition industry which clearly recognize the significance of knowledge synergy and the development of competencies. For a detailed description of this approach, see den Hertog *et al.* (2000).

A Knowledge-Based Framework — Reinventing Industry Boundaries

To create the roadmap for the future growth of a company, the corporate strategy needs to adhere to several strategic conditions (Parmar *et al.*, 2014). From an industry point of view the company's behavior is typified by certain change-provoking behavioral traits. These can be manifested in a:

- Change, in some fundamental way, to the rules of engagement in a long-standing industry.
- Redrawing of the boundaries between current and adjacent industries.
- And (or) creating of entirely new industries or industry approaches with value-creating propositions. This value may arise from new combinations, namely aligning adjacent competencies, technologies or even actively scouting emerging business areas.

In understanding the change in business models and the innovation drivers, Parmar *et al.* (2014) refer to several (complementary) strategy levels of questioning.

The first level of questioning is a competency-based viewpoint and considers the core competencies, enabling competencies and exploration of new competency and assets. It addresses the company roadmap with which to make a company's position distinctive and to enter new businesses and markets. The second level of questioning is about the customer focus. What is the company's attitude towards customer centricity and how do companies conduct activities to gain intelligence about

Table 1. Overview of strategy approach to reinventing industry boundaries (Parmar *et al.*, 2014).

Strategy framework	*Ultimate question*
Competency based	*How can we build on the capabilities and assets that already make us distinctive to enter new businesses and markets?*
Customer focus	*What does a close study of customers' behavior tell us about their tacit, unmet needs?*
Business environment change	*If we follow "megatrends" or other shifts to their logical conclusion, what future business opportunities will become clear?*
Create value from knowledge	*How can we create value for customers using knowledge, data and analytic tools we own or could have access to?*

customers' behavior and how to define their unmet needs? The third level of questioning refers to the changes in the business environment. How do companies absorb changes in the environment, how do they grasp society trends and the global effects for their businesses? This is all about plotting the roadmap and ascertaining the "blue ocean strategy" with which to identify relevant business opportunities. This final level of questioning, e.g. the knowledge-based framework, addresses the question of value creation by means of internal R&D development, knowledge creation or finding access to relevant knowledge and technologies.

A brief look (see Table 2) at the companies on their corporate strategy and fulfillment of the business conditions provides a first impression of the company's attitude. Each company changed in some fundamental way the rules of engagement in a long-standing industry. DSM changed the rules of the game in the chemicals sector, and provided evidence to leverage

Table 2. Overview of company characteristics of the industry leaders.

Company	Organization	Company leadership characteristics
Royal DSM	• DSM is an international company and one of Europe's market leaders in the chemical and pharmaceutical industry. The company is listed on NYSE Euronext. • DSM incorporates 23,500 employees who deliver annual net sales of €9,131 billion in 2012 (compared to €9,048 billion in 2011) and a net profit of €437 million in 2012. This sales volume is generated by four DSM Divisions: Nutrition, Pharmaceuticals, Performance Materials and Polymer Intermediates.	• Industry leader in chemicals and active in life sciences and materials sciences. • DSM is characterized as a global science-based company active in health, nutrition and materials. DSM's mission is to "create brighter lives for people today and generations to come" by connecting its unique competencies in life sciences and materials sciences. DSM is driving economic prosperity, environmental progress and social advances to create sustainable value for all stakeholders. • Parallel to the four division clusters the DSM innovation center reported an autonomous sales volumes of €102 million in 2012, compared to €60 million in 2011, an increase of 60%.

(*Continued*)

Table 2. (*Continued*)

Company	Organization	Company leadership characteristics
High Tech Campus Eindhoven	• High Tech Campus Eindhoven is the "smartest km^2" in the Netherlands with more than 120 companies and institutes, and some 8,000 researchers, developers and entrepreneurs working on future technologies and products. • High Tech Campus Eindhoven helps firms to accelerate innovation by offering easy access to high-tech facilities and international networks. • High Tech Campus Eindhoven companies like Philips, NXP, IBM and Intel are resident on High Tech Campus Eindhoven and strategically decide what knowledge, skills and R&D facilities they share in order to achieve faster, better and more customer-oriented innovation.	• High Tech Campus Eindhoven is located at the heart of Europe's leading R&D region. • Located in the Brainport region of the Netherlands, High Tech Campus Eindhoven companies are responsible for nearly 50% of all Dutch patent applications. • High Tech Campus Eindhoven acts as a powerful R&D cluster and open innovation ecosystem, where research activities lead to new business creation. • High Tech Campus Eindhoven was voted by *Fortune* in 2012 as one of the top-seven locations in the world when it comes to opportunities for innovative start-up businesses. Furthermore the region of Eindhoven received the Intelligent Community Forum (ICF) award for "smartest region of the world" in 2011.

(*Continued*)

Table 2. (*Continued*)

Company	Organization	Company leadership characteristics
Newtricious	• Newtricious is a Dutch life sciences company, and works together in partnerships with leading scientists, innovative companies, organizations and public authorities. The roots of the company remain in the entrepreneurial spirit of the market-leading company specialized in the production and distribution of eggs.	• Leader in agriculture and connecting competencies in nutrition and life sciences. • Since 1998, Globus Egg has led the European market with 8% of the total production in market sales. The Netherlands is the world's number one exporter, distributing at large volumes. • CEO started Newtricious in 2006 with the aim of developing a new generation of specialized nutrition, which contribute to a better health and well-being.
Janssen Pharmaceutical companies of Johnson & Johnson	• Janssen Pharmaceutical companies is a part of the Johnson & Johnson corporation, one of the largest and most well-respected healthcare corporations in the world. Johnson & Johnson is active in more than 60 countries and incorporates over 250 sister companies.	• Industry leader in pharmaceutical industry. • In 2011 its pharmaceutical R&D expenditures were \$5,136 million, equivalent to 21.1% of sales in the pharmaceutical segment of Johnson & Johnson. Pharmaceutical R&D expenditures for the year 2012 were \$5,362 million, equivalent to 21.2% of sales in the pharmaceutical segment of Johnson & Johnson.

(*Continued*)

Table 2. (*Continued*)

Company	Organization	Company leadership characteristics
	• Johnson & Johnson entails three healthcare business groups: the Janssen Group (like prescriptive medicines and diagnostics, or medicines in areas of neurodegenerative diseases, oncology, cardiovascular, immunology, infectious diseases), Consumer Products (like skin care and baby products), and Medical Devices & Diagnostics (like hip and knee replacements, sterilization products, disposable contact lenses). • All pharmaceutical activities of Johnson & Johnson are bundled together under the name "Janssen Pharmaceutical companies."	• Janssen's strategic goal for the year 2020 is ambitious: to be number one in five therapeutic areas. • On a global scale, 70% of its sales are from products that are number one or number two in global market share. • Approximately two-thirds of the growth over the past ten years has come from organic growth tied to innovation, with the balance coming from licensing, partnerships and acquisitions. • The annual Access to Medicine Index of 2012 positions Johnson & Johnson as a rising star and gives it second place in the ranking (rated ninth in 2010).

upon their brand promise: "Bright Science. Brighter Living.™" Newtricious performed award-winning research with the goal of developing knowledge and secure health claims. A roadmap of entrepreneurship in nutrition and life sciences was performed by a company (Newtricious) originating from an agricultural background. High Tech Campus Eindhoven created an entirely new industry approach for the high-tech sector by designing an ecosystem for cooperation, new ventures, start-ups and innovation.

The knowledge development process in R&D, seizing new growth opportunities and core competencies, will be a field of discussion in each case study chapter. The systems view of organizational learning is especially relevant here. The underlying thought is that there is a constant change of the knowledge needed by the organization. Apart from continuous change of the product, service or accompanying process or technology, constant movement (change of place) is another essential characteristic of knowledge. Knowledge flows from one development department or organizational unit to the other, from developers to users, from unit to unit, from emerging business area to the existing market divisions, from outside to the inside of the organization, back and forth.

Each of the cases presented in the following chapters considers the above-mentioned strategic questions and the topics of the business model, the value-creation strategy, and the accompanying organization design. Each business case is introduced by the leading management questions and is basically an exercise in sense making. The basic question is to find out "What is the story here?" How has something become an event like that? What does this mean, and what action has been sensible? The concept of the business model (Magretta, 2001) of a firm is captured by the answers to the following questions: Who is the customer? What does the customer value? How does the enterprise make money in this business? Each business case is described and introduced by the leading management questions. We address:

- The business model and the value creation strategy.
- The customer and market perspective of the business strategy.

- The role of innovation.
- The accompanying organization (re)design.
- The competency and R&D strategies aimed at creating added value.

Those are the questions we should ask ourselves all the time. The business model (or business logic) is not a synonym for "business strategy." Basically, the model shows how a firm creates knowledge, creates value and makes money. It is the firm's own (and often unique) way of implementing a strategy: the combination of the right commercial, organizational and technological elements. However, the answers to the four levels of questioning are not sufficient for the understanding of business innovation. Knowledge about the context (society, sustainability, technology etc.) in which the firm operates is also indispensable. The context of the environment, the market, stakeholders and contingencies is also relevant. Furthermore, we have regarded the cases within perspective timeframe, looking at the change process in which the firm is involved, in order to ascertain a view of the "whole transformation story." The dynamics of the cases are interesting as well. This includes myriad of things, including the process, the starting point, earlier problems, effects of earlier policies, present challenges, expectations for the future etc. In this way our understanding of business models can reach beyond merely listing best practices and success factors.

Metamorphosis — The Leading Questions of the Knowledge Enterprise

Effective managers and professionals in organizations have developed the capacity to "read" situations. At the back of their minds they think out various scenarios and their associated action patterns. They are aware that new insights arise by reading the situation from a different perspective. They are open minded and flexible, and are able to postpone judgement as long as the image in their mind is incomplete; and they are aware that new insight into a situation does not arise until they look at problems through a different pair of glasses. This book offers that very new pair of glasses: the perspective of business transformation, innovation and value creation, and the actual, intriguing management practices of global knowledge enterprises.

In the next chapter we examine the successful business transformations of international companies in a range of businesses including those working in the chemical, pharmaceutical, healthcare, nutrition and hightech industries. Each case is accompanied by the leading questions on transforming the organization.

In some companies, this development takes place as a transformation; planned, learning-by-doing. In some companies this development seems like a true revolution. Firms that were known as being "steady" five or ten years ago have undergone a metamorphosis that only a few people would have believed possible. But when reading the company stories one will find out another driver for this model change. The commitment to transforming into an organization embracing open innovation and desire for social engagement are also motivating factors. When organizations operate consciously from a model of innovation, the transformation of the entire business system works well. We observed that the innovation initiatives, the combination of steady state management with room for change, provide a valuable path for growth.

Let us briefly look at the leading management questions of each corporate story:

- Royal DSM's ability to change as a core competency. The leading question: how should core competencies be redesigned and how should strategic choices be made on innovation and R&D capabilities to generate consistent growth?
- High Tech Campus Eindhoven becoming positioned as an innovation hotspot and being the "smartest region of the world." The leading question: how can the ecosystem for open innovation flourish in the high-tech sector? How to create a powerful R&D cluster, become one of the largest science parks in the world and design a successful model for open innovation?
- Janssen Pharmaceutical companies of Johnson & Johnson. An international corporation moving frontiers and solving patients' unmet medical needs. The leading question: how does a thought and global market leader in the development of pharmaceuticals transform its knowledge organization in search of breakthroughs in therapeutic competencies?
- Newtricious, a European leader in agriculture, exploring the discovery of the ultimate value of eggs and managing the knowledge chain from agriculture to nutrition. The leading question: how does a European market leader in the production and distribution of egg products transform into a knowledge enterprise in the food nutrition and life sciences segment?

What do these examples show? They show the focus on customer demands, quality procedures, cash flow and internal streamlining of processes, but moreover they do not overlook one crucial factor: the *knowledge factor*. This is the knowledge not only needed to keep the processes going and to improve them continuously, but also the knowledge required to safeguard the company position in the future. Knowledge that can be used to explore new opportunities and keep competitors at a distance.

These companies have understood that their business model is vulnerable to the drivers of value erosion. The companies are constantly fighting the law of value erosion. Products, technologies, patents, and services exchanged in the global market gradually lose value from the moment they are introduced in that market. Imitation and the introduction of new and better alternatives are the most important drivers of this value erosion. But institutional change and the opening of global markets (transparency) can also play a major role. To counter value erosion, these firms have found other and new ways of value creation. The companies we interviewed seem dedicated, even persistent, in sustained leveraging of their core competencies. They are in a constant process to adapt the strategy and the structure to meet the business demands.

This is a crucial, insightful and intriguing perspective. We observed companies and networks of companies that have transformed their business model successfully to meet new industry conditions. The next chapter presents the company case studies, which serve to illustrate the development of the knowledge enterprise of European and global market leaders and international network organizations. We explore the recent management practices of international firms in the global markets, which expand their market borders and enter new emerging market areas.

While we present good practices, it is not the intention to present best practices cases. Real changes and transformations cannot take place by merely copying best practices. Organizational innovation is predominantly a learning process that requires inspiration, insight, evidence from consistent management and recognition. Among the learning process these companies encounter:

- The lesson of consistently searching for new growth opportunities mixed with the dedication towards sustainable growth.
- The need to keep focussing on the challenges posed in their business model.
- The absorptive capacity to keep up with global trends on energy, aging population and healthcare.
- The dedication to adopt the trends and convert them to solutions for challenging consumer and population needs, and solutions for healthcare, energy and climate control conditions.
- Managing the paradox of structure and strategy. Managing the new demands on the organization of innovation.

Chapter 3

Design and Implementation of Innovation — Royal DSM: Ability to Change as a Core Competency

The leading question

We examine the successful business transformation of an international chemical company made in order to manage innovation in a multiple range of businesses including chemicals, healthcare, nutrition and materials. How should core competencies be redesigned and how should strategic choices be made on innovation and R&D capabilities to generate consistent growth?

Company profile

Royal DSM is an international company and one of Europe's market leaders in the chemical and pharmaceutical industry with four division clusters (see Fig. 1). The company is listed on the NYSE Euronext. DSM is characterized as a global science-based company active in health, nutrition and materials. DSM's mission is to "create brighter lives for people today and generations to come" by connecting its unique competencies in life sciences and materials sciences. DSM is

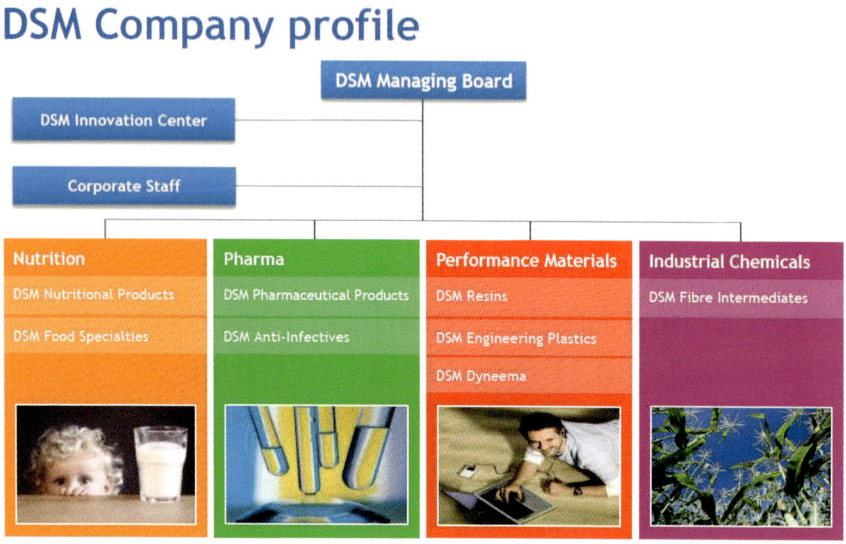

Fig. 1. DSM company profile. Reproduced with permission of Royal DSM.

driving economic prosperity, environmental progress and social advances to create sustainable value for all stakeholders. DSM delivers innovative solutions that nourish, protect and improve performance in global markets such as food and dietary supplements, personal care, feed, pharmaceuticals, medical devices, automotive, paints, electrical and electronics, life protection, alternative energy and bio-based materials. DSM incorporates 23,500 employees who deliver annual net sales of €9,131 billion in 2012 (compared to €9,048 billion in 2011) and a net profit of €437 million in 2012. This sales volume is generated by four DSM Divisions: Nutrition, Pharma, Performance Materials and Polymer Intermediates. Parallel to the four Division Clusters the DSM innovation center reported an autonomous sales volumes of €102 million in 2012, compared to €60 million in 2011, an increase of 60%.

In the course of its history of more than 100 years, DSM has consistently demonstrated the ability to adapt to a new

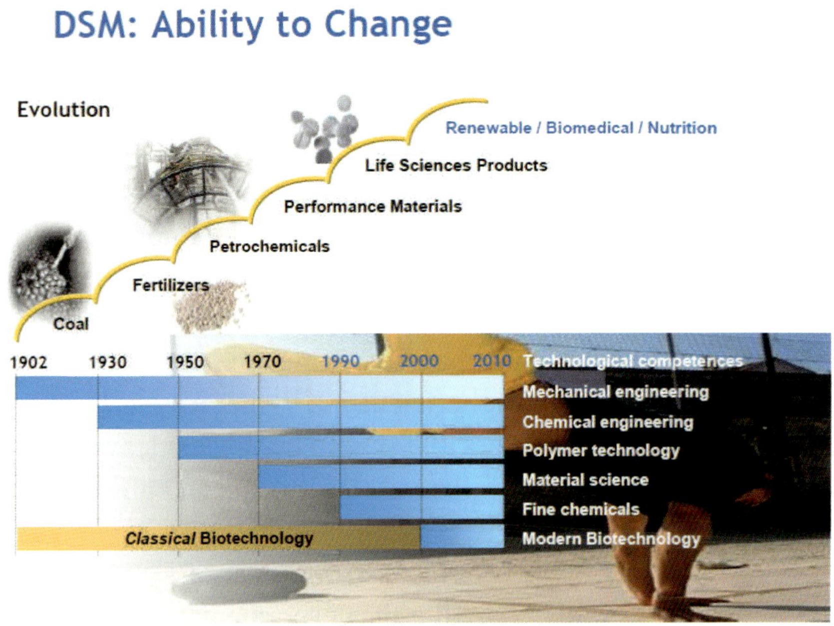

Fig. 2. DSM's horizon of successive transformations. Reproduced with permission of Royal DSM.

business horizon and transform into a knowledge enterprise (see Fig. 2). Originally a coal mining firm from 1900 until the 1930s, DSM started to shift its focus to chemicals when an opportunity arose in 1930 to produce fertilizer on a large scale, based on coal by-products. DSM's company horizon stretched and in the process of evolution capitalized new opportunities, passing through phases which included fertilizers and petrochemicals, before moving towards performance materials. Over the decades, DSM has been guided by its corporate mission, strategic foresight on its core business and innovation strategy, to transform its knowledge structure. By the end of the 1970s, the company was well known for its bulk chemical business, which provided a turning point for the knowledge infrastructure of DSM. Performance materials and life sciences became new areas of business and DSM adapted its knowledge towards these core domains. DSM turned its technological competencies from mechanical and chemical engineering to materials, polymers and fine chemicals. Year by year the company built up and integrated new competencies in biotechnology and fermentation processes along with expertise in microbiology, organic chemistry and process technology (e.g. Gist-Brocades (den Hertog & Huizenga, 2000)). Today DSM is positioned as a global life sciences and materials sciences company, communicating the brand promise of "Bright Science. Brighter Living.™" This company vision is leveraged by its core competencies and concentrates on the strategic pillars of (i) nutrition and pharmaceuticals (life sciences); and (ii) materials sciences.

This organization (Fig. 2) is characteristic of DSM's transformation. Constantly changing the corporate path is grounded in the roots of the company through:

- Strategic foresight.
- A strategic focus to understand and respond to global trends.
- An enduring commitment to its core competencies.
- An innovation climate: a science-based culture and advocacy for scientific breakthroughs.
- A supporting governance structure for the knowledge enterprise.

Strategic focus dominated by global trends

Between 2000 and 2013, the strategy of DSM was marked by five-year strategic programs to direct vision and focus (Table 1). In 2000, for example, the "Vision 2005" program concentrated on the turnaround from bulk to specialties. During the following period, in the "Vision 2010" program, the strategic theme was to build on the strengths that the company had gained in previous

Table 1. Strategies for the transformation of the company.

Year Initiative	Knowledge strategy	Focus areas for growth
2000	**"Vision 2005:" Focus and Value**	Strategic program focussed on transforming the portfolio from bulk chemicals into specialties.
2005	**"Vision 2010:" Building on Strengths**	Strategic program focussed on reaping further rewards from the company's portfolio transformation which took place from 2000 to 2005.
2010	**DSM "in motion:" Driving focussed growth**	Marking the shift from an era of intensive portfolio management to a knowledge strategy of maximizing sustainable, profitable growth.

years. This was accompanied by strong portfolio management and preparation for the next steps. DSM's "in motion" program (of 2010) was initiated when the company gained control of its portfolio of competencies and projects. The company was organized for the next level in sustainable growth.

DSM's current strategic focus is a response to three major global trends that the company has identified:

- Global shifts: a global demographic shift of wealth from West to East and from North to South, as well as a trend towards an increasingly older, increasingly urban, increasingly connected, and increasingly wealthy global population.
- Climate and energy: new, major challenges in the field of climate and energy.
- Health and well-being: a growing interest in answering the societal question of how to secure health and wellness for all.

These trends are incorporated in DSM's focussed growth strategy for providing solutions.

Strategic initiatives at DSM to leverage on "Bright Science. Brighter Living.™"

Keeping in mind these trends and the growth ambitions, one can foresee several challenges. In their corporate vision, DSM emphasizes value creation in combination with the "triple P" principle: the primary goal is the creation of sustainable shared value for all stakeholders based on innovations that benefit people, planet and profit. DSM's triple P statement is defined by:

- People: Together with customers we make the lives of everyday people brighter; as well as nurturing a global DSM Team of 23,500 people who are motivated to make a difference every day.
- Planet: Society and the planet derive benefits from the impact of more sustainable, longer-lasting, safer, healthier and more nutritious products, processes and practices.
- Profit: Our shareholders and stakeholders benefit from stronger growth and profitability based on long-term success.

Seven principles for organizational dynamics in the knowledge infrastructure

The transformation of DSM rests upon several capabilities: scalability; need for speed; and managing emerging business areas. Scalability is the ability to integrate new competencies, mergers and acquisitions, and the ability to up-scale this knowledge and these competencies for use within the DSM divisions. Speed requires the organizational capability to rapidly integrate external knowledge into the R&D organization and business processes. A great deal of DSM's innovation within existing business sectors takes place through incremental innovations within said sectors. In addition CIO Rob van Leen argues[1] that the cornerstone for "making money with innovation" also resides in the emerging business areas, which are the most important tools for innovation in new platforms. This entails the management, scouting out and nourishing of emerging business areas. It is the appointed responsibility of an innovation center unit to guide DSM to growth in new markets with new technological competencies.

Steering and controlling the knowledge infrastructure of DSM requires an intelligent governance structure. This structure is steered and controlled by the DSM's CTO, Marcel Wubbolts, and the CIO, Rob van Leen. Layer by layer, this governance structure ensures the execution of DSM's knowledge vision. There are several organizational instruments implemented, which support the knowledge flows in the DSM organization. We will see that the organizational model at DSM consists of a coherent set of measures, which clearly show a competency orientation. This knowledge infrastructure and competency orientation is primarily managed by seven key organizational instruments, ensuring a lateral flow of knowledge within the organization:

1. The portfolio of core competencies and "know-how to scale."
2. The strategic council.
3. The guidance by the core competency area plan.
4. A corporate science council and its knowledge principles.
5. A DSM science network model.
6. The central business role for the innovation center.

[1] All unreferenced quotes are taken from interviews held with the respective companies at their company headquarters during 2012 and 2013.

7. The growth areas and management of the emerging business areas.

Know-how and the ability to scale — the R&D strategy

The full integration of Gist-Brocades and competencies in the sphere of enzymes and process technology in the period between 1998 and 2002 has given DSM a competitive advantage. Marcel Wubbolts, DSM's CTO remarks: "... we fully integrated these competencies in biotechnology, pharmaceutical syntheses and process technology in the core R&D competencies, which enabled us to develop faster and better fitting solutions ..."

The future agenda of the CTO's strategy is to identify and act upon technological trends. The most recent trends include:

- Food and nutrition security — enabling the availability of the right amount and quality of food.
- Health — innovations in both preventive as well as curative care.
- Energy security — enabling the availability of a sustainable energy supply.
- Sustainable manufacturing and materials security — providing materials resources in a circular, closed loop, mode of operation.

DSM is keen to keep focussing on its portfolio of core competencies. The corporate R&D strategy is responsible for managing a focussed portfolio of core competencies:

- Biotechnology.
- Advanced synthetic methods (organic chemicals).
- Process technology.
- Materials sciences.

- Materials chemistry.
- Nutrition.
- Analyses and measurement.

Managing and safeguarding the competency landscape is the joint responsibility of the corporate research and the business groups. Based on consistent and long-term planning, and the commitment and joint efforts of the people from research and the business, DSM is steering its competency portfolio. The strategic council is the lateral instrument used to safeguard this knowledge process and manage the core competency development.

The strategic council — guiding the core competency development

Innovation, as per DSM's definition, is more than just R&D. The corporate R&D expenditure for central R&D is 10% of the total budget. R&D turns cash into know-how, ideas and intellectual property (IP) for DSM. The other 90% of the R&D budget is allocated to strengthening competencies in order to serve the existing business lines. It also helps to support the sales of the business groups with incremental innovation. These innovations include small steps to improve products, and tackle bottlenecks in customer sites or in the production process and so forth. Most importantly, though, these innovations turn know-how into new business, and thus into new cash. Safeguarding the competency landscape is a joint responsibility of corporate research, primarily responsible for the mid term and long term, and the business groups, responsible for the short term. Aligning their objectives and activities requires good management attention. The strategic council manages this playing field, in which all R&D directors of the business groups are members, chaired by the CTO. Marcel Wubbolts, DSM's CTO, remarks: "... the strategic council overlooks the strategic developments in the DSM business groups. This strategy match ensures the possibilities to develop and share competencies between business groups . . ." Biotechnology, for example, is applied in nutrition, pharmaceuticals, materials science in one of the emerging business areas (EBA), bio-based products and services. This leverages the competency position and the investments made therein. Competencies that are primarily applied by one group, e.g. the nutrition competency in the DNP nutritional products group, are the responsibility of that same group. Corporate research supports the competency developments that can lead to entirely new businesses or can be shared between different groups. The corporate research program also addresses the trends and needs of the EBAs and the global business incubator (both part of the innovation center).

The strategic council's primary role is of a strategic nature and it operates across organizational boundaries (lateral development). It decides on the ownership of topics between the business groups and the corporate research role. The council has to keep track of the internal technological development, the business needs, and the external developments. The range of council discussions includes:

- Public–private partnerships.
- Top sector policy (technological developments).
- Technology subsidy programs and technology clusters.
- Trends in the society.
- External developments like DSM China's innovation center: its regional opportunities and the accompanying knowledge network.
- Trending topics like food and nutrition security, and energy security.

The master plan for competency development

The strategic council has meetings up to six times a year. The council works on the basis of a competency area plan, with a yearly update and a long-term plan of five years. The competency plan comprises several competency needs within DSM. It is a solid mixture of the business needs, for which information is gathered by the corporate scientists in their discussions with the business groups (internal clients). Furthermore, the (unaddressed) needs of the R&D population in DSM, and the assessment by the corporate scientists of their view of the external developments, are included. These are the main factors involved in the competency area plan, which, in turn, is the basis for much of the R&D activities performed in the organization. For example, one of the global trends and business needs is biotech, so the plan includes these trends, e.g. in food, nutrition, and materials sciences. The plan describes the business-to-business (B2B) needs, the current strengths, and the requirements for investments to fill the gaps. The master plan is funded by the corporate research budget, the business group, or by joint funding.

Corporate science council

Another part of the DSM knowledge infrastructure is the crucial role of the scientists. The corporate science council consists of the professors and principal scientists of DSM. The R&D directors are not part of this council. This organizational corporate entity discusses the research programs and is dedicated to scouting out new research areas of interest on a global scale. This lateral organization unit both strengthens the existing R&D competencies and dedicates itself to developing new competencies.

Developing the talent pool — the assignment of the resource council

The resource council looks at the talents in the DSM science population. The objectives of the council address the human resources management topics:

- Locate the crucial skills, people, and talents flowing in the DSM organization.
- Decide how to rotate the skills and expertise in the organization.
- Plan how to nurture and develop the talent pool by, for example, career development and succession planning.

The resource council has a crucial role in the knowledge enterprise of DSM. The talents are the carriers of knowledge, knowledge that is scarce and extremely important. If such people were to exit the organization, this would hurt the knowledge system. The council's role is to attract and retain these knowledge carriers. By means of a "blueprint," the council manages what skills and competencies DSM needs, which people obtain these capabilities and skills, and which succession planning belongs to these key skills. The council's role also includes the development component. The standard profile of an R&D worker is now very different from that of ten years ago. A key trend is improving the skills of the science people is communication, which is seen as increasingly important, both in the technical audience as well as in the business audience. In the development of the talent pool, several instruments are used:

- Sending people to conferences.
- People management training.
- Communication training.

DSM innovation center — where technology meets the emerging business opportunities

For DSM, innovation is not only a matter of science and technology, but also of organizing the innovation process across the firm's boundaries. Both the division boundaries and the external boundaries apply, e.g. upcoming markets, external knowledge, technology development and companies outside DSM. A central role is dedicated to the innovation center, headed by CIO Rob van Leen. This organizational unit has two major innovation roles (see Fig. 3):

- Creating new business in areas that are outside the scope of the existing business groups, through scouting and managing the EBAs.
- Accelerating innovation throughout the company. This is, amongst others, achieved through the Excellence in Innovation learning curriculum, support in the fields of licensing

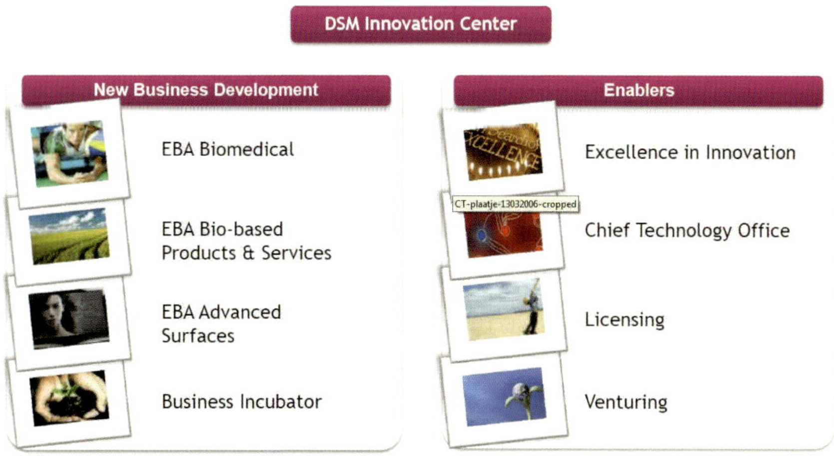

Fig. 3. DSM innovation center — key roles for innovation. Reproduced with permission of Royal DSM.

and venturing and the corporate research program, run by the CTO.

The DSM innovation center and the role of the CIO were established in 2006 with the ambition of transforming DSM into an intrinsically innovative company. In particular, this organizational movement contributed to transforming DSM (van Leen, 2010) from a risk-averse, technology-push orientation towards:

- Incorporating customer needs.
- Sophisticated market orientation.
- A breeding ground for innovative entrepreneurial activities.

EBAs — raison d'être *for growth*

Rob van Leen, explains: "In the Corporate Strategy Dialogues, performed once every 5 years, DSM decided to re-engineer the innovation function. Four EBAs were established to secure DSM's long-term innovative growth . . ." These initial EBAs resided in the domains of industrial biotechnology, biomedical materials, personalized nutrition and specialty packaging. With the EBAs, DSM introduced a consistent platform for exploring new business opportunities in life sciences and materials sciences. The *raison d'être* for the emerging business areas was a mix of arguments:

- Re-engineer the corporate business development such that it possesses an incubator function.
- Create a more cohesive project portfolio instead of solo, valuable projects.
- Start innovative activities outside the scope of the existing business groups, based upon the major trends.
- Create more impact for the long term and nurture innovation outside the operational, daily business routines.

- Introduce open innovation through a host of projects and initiatives, to prevent the "not-invented-here" syndrome.

By the end of 2010, the results of the four EBAs were evaluated. Two EBAs were successful in meeting the growth, competency and financial objectives. These two EBAs created value and new knowledge. The other EBAs created new knowledge and value, but were reconsidered in respect of the growth strategy. Considering the long-term path of DSM and the goals of the innovation center, it was thought these knowledge initiatives would fare better outside the DSM context and were actually transferred to external parties. In managing the portfolio of the EBAs, DSM is controlling its future growth and, at the same time, aligning its competency portfolio. In doing the right things the right way, the innovation center scouts and evaluates the EBAs. In essence, the EBAs are the *raison d'être* for DSM growth. Starting and investing in a new EBA is a matter of good management consideration. A new EBA may arise based on the DSM's search to address relevant long-term trends, e.g. food and nutrition security, health, energy and raw materials security. For example, in 2010, a new presence in an EBA was formed: DSM advanced surfaces, focussing on solar applications.

An example of an EBA — biomedical materials

Development in one particular EBA, biomedical materials, was started in 2006 with a few people and a handful of ideas. By the end of 2010, it had grown into a considerable pipeline of developed products, with 150 people working in the area and four venturing investments. In 2012, DSM also acquired Kensey Nash Corporation, resulting in a leading position with a very broad product portfolio. This EBA is growing, and is aligned with the envisaged trends of biomedical materials. Stretching the EBA's ambition is one of the targets of the innovation center. The "good to great" ambition (Collins, 2001) is written down in the statement of "becoming a business group of DSM, within ten years." The intentions of the business plan include the change-forcing objectives to have a turnover level of €500 million in the next ten years.

Close interaction of corporate R&D and the innovation center — safeguarding the long-term perspective

The corporate research program and the innovation center work closely together to ensure the long-term success of DSM. This is a critical element in the knowledge infrastructure as they invest in the competencies, which are either one step ahead or one step aside from the current business, and business groups. Previously, innovative ideas within the business groups did not make it to a clear proposal or even a project, and the urgency of daily business conditions sometimes dampened the power and the rise of new ideas. The innovation center's role is to absorb these ideas and, through a formal process, secure funding for them. Among the criteria is the potential of the project to become a synergy project. These are projects which serve multiple business groups, have a clear market link, and (if possible) are cofounded from central R&D and decentralized business groups.

Innovation rules to create knowledge synergy

The innovation center uses explicit guidelines, according to CIO Rob van Leen. These are guidelines to stimulate innovation, amongst which are budget rules and sustainability rules for tracking the innovation process.

- *Research budget rules.* 50% of the Corporate Research program projects and budget has to be linked to more than one of the core competency areas.
- *Sustainability rules.* Innovative new products not only serve as valuable business but also support DSM's sustainability targets. In 2009, close to 80% of the innovations launched were ECO+ solutions, which means that — when considered over their entire life cycle — they offer clear ecological benefits compared to the mainstream solutions with which they compete.
- *The corporate R&D spend.* R&D expenditure on innovation is 10%, which emphasizes the development of competencies for the long term. The other 90% of the R&D budget is allocated to strengthening the competencies to serve the existing business lines.
- *Recognizing sustainability in the innovation pipeline.* Within the innovation process, managed similarly to the staged model (Cooper, 1994), DSM uses a clear range of measurement moments dedicated to sustainability.

Furthermore CIO Rob van Leen states that steering the innovation pipeline is based upon the principles of open innovation (Chesbrough, 2003; Kirschbaum, 2005). This is a shift from a closed R&D model towards an open model (see Fig. 4). Projects can be launched from either internal or external technology sources, and new technology can enter into the process at various stages. In addition, projects can go to market in several ways such as spinoff ventures, licensing in or out of DSM, alongside the existing DSM sales and marketing channels. It describes the

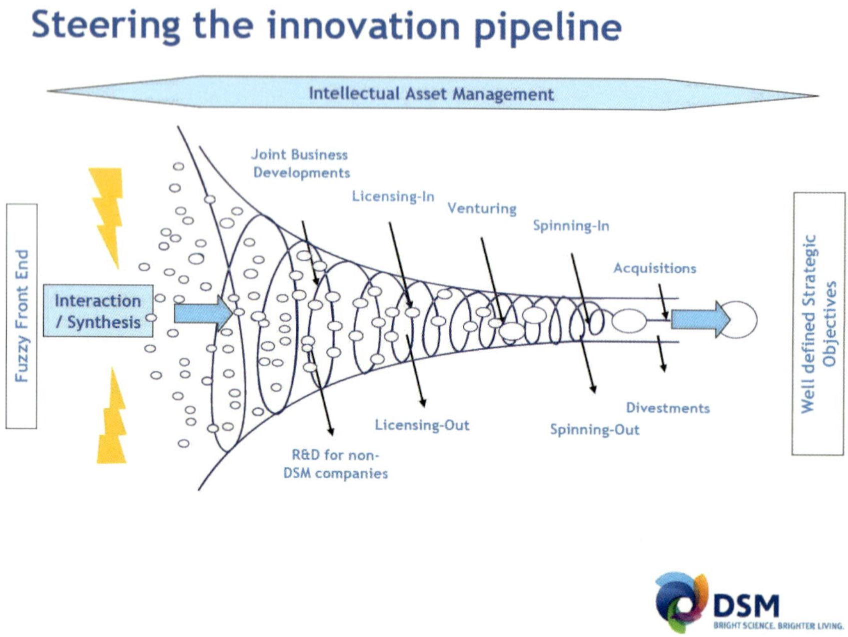

Fig. 4. Steering the DSM innovation pipeline. Reproduced with permission of Royal DSM.

"way we operate around here" to express the working methods for the inflow and outflow of knowledge.

The majority of the DSM business groups decided to step up the green part of their research and technology budgets from 2011 onwards. This has been a major achievement in the five-year period of DSM's "in motion" program. DSM has been one of the leaders in the Dow Jones Sustainability Index for many consecutive years.

Business in transition — lessons learned

Innovation is also a story of coincidences. Metaphorically, it is similar to sports like rugby and American football: the team envisages the end line ahead, but the road to get there is still open. In order to get there, the team makes steps forwards and backwards. Innovation sometimes resembles a rugby approach, where team players jointly proceed forward to the end. Learning from lessons the team has made, the players take a step back, evaluate the investments in resources, and check the market volume and sales which have been created. Amongst these are the exemplary stories of Dyneema® and ®Claryl. Dyneema® is a story about expanding the product horizon and the 2012 Olympic Games.

Dyneema® — the premium brand

Dyneema® is respected as the premium brand for ultra-high-molecular-weight polyethylene (UHMwPE). DSM manufactures and sells products in several forms including fibers, tape, and uni-directional (UD) sheets. The oldest technological and business scenarios were written entirely on structural composites. DSM started with a certain vision and a market perspective and, ten years later, has arrived at quite a different business horizon. Marcel Wubbolts, DSM's CTO explains:

> One single starting point, that's how Dyneema® took off. But if we look back, the lessons learned and the broad horizon of applications made with Dyneema® nowadays... one could not have imagined this upfront... it's a huge portfolio of products. This fiber technology is inserted in areas of life protection, heavy industry, performance textiles but also in biomedical.

The first commercial order of Dyneema® was from a cloth-braiding factory which was present in the sports sector. Sport has remained a key sector for Dyneema®, but, in terms of volume and value, other sectors have also appeared, including marine, life protection, and cutresistant gloves for the industrial sector. Dyneema® is used in multiple application areas, e.g. in performance textiles. One of the landmarks was the 2012 Olympics Games in London, where the Dyneema® fibers were used extensively in the ultra-modern cycling suits during the velodrome cycling races.

®*Claryl picture glass*

®Claryl picture glass, exemplifies the coincidence when an idea seems not the biggest seller at first, but "new combinations" result in a breakthrough. Let us consider this as an example of new market discoveries where the lessons learned turned out to be ultimately favorable. DSM had developed an anti-reflective coating for picture glass; a glass that minimizes reflection and enables the viewer to see the pictures without disturbances. Eventually, the first technological direction was discovered, but the market remained relatively small. As a consequence, DSM withdrew from this market. However, the innovation team observed that if you can attach these coatings onto glass plates, for example used in the manufacture of solar panels, they will be more efficient and anti-reflective coatings for solar cells is a huge market. In the first instance, DSM introduced the technology in one market sphere before gradually, when talking with customers, reaching an understanding that the market was not viable. They discovered an alternative market, which was more valuable in the end. DSM would currently not have been present in the solar segment if this had not occurred. DSM's organizational learning capacity proved invaluable to create this market position.

Process thinking as an intangible competency

In addition to the guidelines and the organization model for innovation, there seems to be one key ingredient. It is the story of an intangible knowledge domain, which is resident in the genes of the organization. Most of the innovations start within DSM with a process perspective which involves thinking through and (re)designing what the ideal process will look like. DSM has a strong history in enzymes and process technology and has made this one of its core competencies. How? Let us consider the example of bio-fuels. Coal, oil and natural gas have long been the engine of the world economy, both as energy sources and as raw materials, but they will run out in the coming centuries. The world will have to switch to alternative, renewable, non-fossil-based solutions, due particularly to the needs of a growing and increasingly demanding population. There is one renewable resource that can sustainably supply the world with food, energy, chemicals and materials: biomass. With the help of biotechnology and chemical synthesis, DSM can learn to use this.

Process thinking in action — bio-based advancements

The first generation of bio-fuels has a disadvantage because it is in competition with the food chain. The so-called advanced bio-fuels are primarily based upon the waste from the agricultural feedstock. The technological challenge is to design an optimal process of transforming feedstock into bio-fuels using technologies currently in the market. A crucial aspect in the bio-fuel process is breaking down the fibers of the agricultural feedstock. At this process stage there is a role for enzymes, which can function at high temperatures. In the process enzymes, viscosity, water, and temperature play a crucial role. The heating and cooling, along with an understanding of the process can be very complex. The CTO, Marcel Wubbolts, explains the powerful role of their "process thinking:"

> It's comparable to a bucket full of hay fragments mixed with some water. Stirring is incredibly difficult and sugar molecules that come out even increase the viscosity. At high temperatures viscosity is lower, but at some point you need to cool down to allow ordinary enzymes to work and it transforms like concrete paste. Then you add the enzymes, which should mix. Again stirring is a heavy task, but you do not want to dilute the mix with water since afterwards you should lose the water again. That would be rather inefficient. When we saw how the process worked in molecular detail, we thought: 'It would be ideal if we would have an enzyme that you already administer at a high temperature. Then the mixture is less viscous, the enzymes work faster and bacterial infections can be prevented so that antibiotics are not needed. When the enzyme starts breaking down the fiber the mixture becomes even less viscous and can be better stirred. At a certain moment it is at the ideal temperature for the yeasts in the next step and one can further process the outcomes.' This process thinking is dominant in the R&D choices. So we are going to subsequently develop an enzyme which can work at a higher temperature. Our competitors have not done it this way and have followed a different approach. Our thermo stable enzymes thus provides a sustainability advantage and a process-cost advantage at the same time...

This demonstrates the importance of process thinking, and how crucial it is to have a true understanding of the entire process. Even more import because it is a key success factor for DSM. Why? It is the key to making technology scalable.

Managing lateral linkages — DSM science network

The R&D organization has a global presence with over 30 different R&D locations: it is a worldwide virtual laboratory. The knowledge system of DSM thrives on bringing people together, scientists and business people, exchanging people and ideas, and executing joint projects, thus creating a true DSM science network. This network model thrives where DSM R&D units link up with one another and share knowledge and competencies for the benefit of the global company. This network philosophy incorporates all people within DSM and the people connected to DSM. The network is similar to a knowledge map; layering the science competencies and people with the external cooperation links to other firms and close ties with research institutes, like MIT in the US and China's research institutes. The DSM science network has a philosophy of sharing, bringing together, and feeling connected and committed to DSM's vision for the future. The network is about trust, partnering, and incorporating firms and people from mergers and acquisitions. The expansion into China was part of the development of DSM's science network. Such regional R&D centers make the most of the opportunities for building partnerships with universities and other research centers in the region.

DSM's focus on high-growth economies (HGEs) has resulted in the establishment of labs and an innovation center in Shanghai, China, and a boost in sales in the HGEs from roughly 22% of overall sales in 2005 to 39% in 2011. DSM expects a large percentage of its growth in the period up to 2015 to come from these HGEs.

Investing in HGEs is one way in which DSM leverages its capabilities: a local presence enables the company to seek and develop talent and competencies with a more natural fit to these markets. DSM has opened three research labs in China — including the DSM China campus headquartered in Zhangjiang Hi-Tech Park in Pudong New Area, Shanghai — as well as partnering in nine joint ventures and establishing 16 wholly-owned foreign enterprises, two branch companies, and five branch offices, employing over 4,000 people in total.

Fruitflow® — sustainable innovations at the crossing borders

The common denominator for DSM is sustainable innovation at the crossing borders of high-performance materials, food and pharmaceuticals. In its search for new discoveries, DSM made a strategic investment in the knowledge of a start-up, Fruitflow®. A small biotech start-up in the UK, called Provexis, discovered a way of unlocking the benefits of tomatoes on cardiovascular activity. In 2008, DSM heard about the idea and liked it enough to invest some seed money into the start-up company through the venturing subsidiary of the innovation center. The investment was fully in line with DSM's strategy to further expand into ingredients for functional food and dietary supplements, focussing on cardiovascular and digestive health. Subsequently, DSM collaborated with Provexis on the marketing and sales, signing for the exclusive distribution role for this product. This collaboration gave Provexis access to a large distribution network in a market where it is important that the products are delivered by known, reliable players. At the same time DSM got access to this very innovative product. The result was Fruitflow®: a unique tomato extract that increases cardiovascular health, is highly sustainable, and aims to help people live longer and healthier lives. Fruitflow® appears to be a breakthrough ingredient as it is the first natural, scientifically substantiated solution contributing to healthy bloodflow.

Managing acquisitions

The knowledge system of DSM thrives on bringing people together, exchanging people and ideas, and find missing competencies. In the past few years, DSM has made several strategic

Table 2. Recent knowledge acquisitions by DSM.

Company	Year	Type of knowledge acquisition
POET	2012	Joint venture with a bio-ethanol producer aim is to use the waste of agricultural feed crop.
Kensey Nash Corporation	2012	Biomedical acquisition.
Ocean Nutrition Canada, ONC	2012	Nutrition acquisition to gain market position and technology.
Tortuga	2012	Nutrition acquisition for minerals in cattle feeds, Brazil.
Martek Biosciences Corporation	2011	Acquisition of leading innovator of products based on microbial and fermentation research.

acquisitions (see Table 2) in this area. As part of its growth strategy, DSM frequently enters into partnerships with companies or organizations possessing competencies in fields where the company intends to grow. The merger and acquisition (M&A) strategy's focus is on nutrition and new, bio-based fuels. Such partnerships are a way of pooling knowledge and resources, meanwhile providing DSM with a window of opportunity. One key lesson learned over the past years is the ability of the DSM organization to absorb external knowledge by means of partnerships and a culture of trust.

One example, from 2011, is DSM's acquisition of Martek Biosciences Corporation, a leading innovator of products based on microbial and fermentation research. The technology platform and research engine that Martek possessed created synergy between both companies. It gave DSM access to scientists with competencies in developing algae- and fungal-based substances, which are primarily used in baby formula. Martek's near- and long-term pipeline also included robust research projects into other applications of industrial biotechnology.

From serendipity towards finding breakthroughs

The bottom line is that DSM has managed a consistent innovation path from 2000 onwards. It has built upon the innovation lessons throughout the years and incorporated the innovation genes from companies such as Gist-Brocades. DSM has successfully managed to transform from a model of "serendipity in innovation" toward a new business model for innovation with a strong directing role for the innovation center, smart core competency development, and a lateral organizational model. This has rotated the organization and transformed the "way we operate around here" approach into a culture for open innovation, venturing, and a structured approach to EBAs.

DSM proves to be a thought leader in its industry and knowledge enterprise, built upon a business transformation. Their roadmap provides evidence to leverage upon its brand promise: "Bright Science. Brighter Living.™"

As Rob van Leen summarizes:

> Our intentions with the establishment of the innovation center definitely have materialized. What started as a kind of experiment has turned into serious business. The innovation center has driven the change in the way innovation is being done at DSM. From an unstructured process, innovation has become a way of living in our company. Innovation is in our genes!

Chapter 4

Design and Implementation of Innovation — Transformations of the Value Chain

High Tech Campus Eindhoven — Innovation in the Hub and the "Smartest Region of the World"

The leading questions

How can the ecosystem for open innovation flourish in the high-tech sector? How is it possible to create a powerful research and development (R&D) cluster, become one of the largest science parks in the world and design a successful model for open innovation?

A hotspot and ecosystem for open innovation

High Tech Campus Eindhoven is an open innovation ecosystem and is part of the internationally awarded "smartest region of the world" 2011–2012. It is the "smartest km^2" in the Netherlands with more than 120 companies and institutes and some 8,000 researchers, developers and entrepreneurs working on future technologies and products. High Tech Campus Eindhoven helps firms to accelerate innovation by offering easy access to high-tech facilities and international networks. Companies like Philips, NXP, IBM and Intel are resident on High Tech Campus Eindhoven and strategically decide what knowledge, skills and R&D facilities they share in order to achieve faster, better and more customer-oriented innovation. High Tech Campus Eindhoven includes application fields like health, energy and smart environments. Located at the heart of the Brainport region in the Netherlands, High Tech Campus Eindhoven companies are responsible for nearly 50% of all Dutch patent applications.

High Tech Campus Eindhoven proved successful as a powerful R&D cluster and open innovation ecosystem, where research activities lead to new business creation.

High Tech Campus Eindhoven is located at the heart of Europe's leading R&D region. The Eindhoven, Louvain, Aachen triangle (ELAt) is an area that has acquired a strong European position in micro-electronics, nano-electronics and life sciences. High Tech Campus Eindhoven aims to accelerate innovation by offering easy access to high-tech facilities and international networks. High Tech Campus Eindhoven has developed over the past ten years into a dynamic mix of more than 120 organizations, from global companies and innovative SME businesses via research institutes and service companies right through to techno start-ups. It is part of the International Association of Science Parks (IASP), the worldwide network of science parks and areas of innovation.

High Tech Campus Eindhoven was voted by *Fortune* in 2012 as one of the top-seven locations in the world when it comes to opportunities for innovative start-up businesses. Furthermore the region of Eindhoven received the Intelligent Community Forum (ICF) award for "the world's smartest region" in 2011. These two landmarks provide evidence that the open innovation model is effective. It is striking to see that, apart from Singapore, only European cities and regions feature in the *Fortune* ranking. Not a single American region made it into the top seven. Western Europe seems to lead the way in the world when it comes to creativity, open innovation, providing opportunities for start-ups and helping to develop successful new businesses.

"It's about partnerships and leveraging knowledge,"[1] explains Cees Admiraal, business development director at the High Tech Campus Eindhoven. He remarks: "Open innovation is the cornerstone for the business model at High Tech Campus Eindhoven. High Tech Campus Eindhoven residents are able to leverage their core competencies and investigate ways to speed up their development, using and sharing each other's knowledge. Partnership is a crucial cornerstone of the ecosystem and business model of High Tech Campus Eindhoven. In sharing lab facilities, joining in projects, crossing technological borders and cooperating at an early stage of development High Tech Campus Eindhoven companies partner up and share knowledge and experience."

High Tech Campus Eindhoven management — orchestrating the source of new business

High Tech Campus Eindhoven system is strongly attached to regional and European developments in the high-tech environment. The rapid pace of new technological development implies a continuous flow of new knowledge. The companies and their knowledge workers represent an ever-growing accumulation of knowledge in various fields of technology.

[1] All unreferenced quotes are taken from interviews held with the respective companies at their company headquarters during 2012 and 2013.

High Tech Campus Eindhoven site management has an orchestrating and crucial role in the ecosystem. They have a profound influence. Their role is similar to the orchestral conductor, creating harmony in the performance of the orchestral performance. High Tech Campus Eindhoven site management has a guiding influence in creating connections between corporate, global companies and start-ups. Connecting people, firms and technology domains are guided, even across High Tech Campus Eindhoven boundaries towards Europe, the US and Asia. High Tech Campus Eindhoven is one of the largest science parks worldwide (measured by the number of companies located at each park) and has strong network connections on a global scale.

In this wellspring of knowledge, new business directions appear and new applications are developed like:

- Beds that monitor the health of patients and elderly people.
- Smart medicines that only deliver the active fluid when and where it is needed.
- Revolutionary packaging that displays in real time how fresh the food actually is.
- Gaming computers that create a gaming experience using light, sound, pictures, vibrations and smells.

Open innovation — create value in the knowledge system to collaborate, share and reduce costs

Management theory has embraced the phenomenon of open innovation. Based upon the principles of open innovation, the closed R&D model has been abandoned in favor of an open model, partnering, co-creation and sharing lab environments (Chesbrough *et al.*, 2006; Huizenga, 2004). In an open innovation model projects can be launched from either internal or external technology sources, and new technology can enter into the development process at various stages. In addition, products can go to market in several ways, such as spinoff ventures, licensing in or out the technology. But above all, open innovation is all about collaboration. But why use an open model? It's about the speed and value erosion when doing things one step at a time. With the current speed of technological developments, a single-firm solution is a working model of the past century. Single competencies, i.e. single-produced products, do not create value and become obsolete at a fast rate. Therefore the collaboration aspect of innovation is the credo of the High Tech Campus Eindhoven model. High Tech Campus Eindhoven's credo of "turning technology into business," where institutes, global companies and start-ups join forces. Amongst the shared technical facilities are the Philips Innovation Services. This facility is a cornerstone in the ecosystem of the High Tech Campus Eindhoven high-tech infrastructure. These facilities provide access to amongst others:

- 20,000 m^2 multi-purpose labs.
- Clean rooms, a reliability lab and an electromagnetic compatibility (EMC) center.

Convenience services

Next to this facility, High Tech Campus Eindhoven encompasses convenience services like laboratories for media research, user testing, as well as a high-level ICT network and central purchasing facilities for industrial gases and chemicals.

Ecosystem

High Tech Campus Eindhoven operates like an ecosystem. This ecosystem is characterized by partnerships boosted by the open research programs of technology institutes like Holst Centre, ExperienceLab, EIT ICT labs, and Solliance. Within these institutes programs are conducted with a range of different partners, each of them cooperating according to their own specific strengths in research for new applications. In due course, the individual companies leverage their innovations and use the research results to implement their own applications.

On the power of this ecosystem, Cees Admiraal remarks:

> High Tech Campus Eindhoven companies can make use of this technical infrastructure, without individually having to make the related costly investments. They simply rent whatever they need. This means that even recently started and relatively small R&D companies can have access to state-of-the-art facilities . . .

The vision and mission of High Tech Campus Eindhoven

Well-known examples of an innovation ecosystem are Silicon Valley and the venture models of pharmaceutical companies. Also, in the past technology corporations like Intel, Alcatel and the Bell Labs used this R&D model to accelerate innovations. Even pharmaceutical companies like Merck and Glaxxo based their R&D strategy on this model. They invested in young start-ups, providing resources and budget and harvesting at a later stage from the successes that were born. This model demonstrated to be viable.

This open campus model became the viable new R&D model (Chesbrough, 2003). The vision behind High Tech Campus Eindhoven was to create an open R&D model for the high-tech sector, sourcing a host of small start-up initiatives at the same time. The initiator of High Tech Campus Eindhoven was the technological corporation Philips. The mission was to create a knowledge/business ecosystem. The first step towards this system was to open the Philips R&D labs and research programs to third parties. This mission was furthermore supported by the idea that sharing R&D in a community would substantially lead to more return on R&D. High Tech Campus Eindhoven development with the shared facilities has been successful in the past years because of the breakthrough concept and the "stick to the plan" type of management. A current landmark is the Holst Centre, which occupies a unique position between academic research and product development.

The High Tech Campus Eindhoven hub

On the High Tech Campus Eindhoven site there are over 120 businesses working on the products and technologies of tomorrow. Right from the start one of the objectives of High Tech Campus Eindhoven has been to create a fertile breeding ground for promising young businesses. Start-ups can locate their operations here in dedicated business and technology accelerator buildings where they can make use of all the existing technical research facilities without having to invest in these facilities themselves. In order to nurture an environment for new starters, spinoffs and spinouts of existing companies, High Tech Campus Eindhoven particular focuses on start-up technical companies. Over the past years the target groups like the techno starters, institutes and global companies have been endorsed in the High Tech Campus Eindhoven hub.

The atmosphere of a business accelerator

The facilities serve both as a business accelerator and as a wellspring for the young entrepreneurs and start-ups to inspire and encourage one another. Besides this infrastructure the campus heartbeat favors an informal, tacit atmosphere that breathes innovation. The ecosystem favors the climate for relevant financial partners and investors, as well as the tacit knowledge of technical talent. Over the past few years the knowledge system of High Tech Campus Eindhoven has broadened and deepened by absorbing technical specialists attracted by the technological challenges. The proximity to a number of universities of technology and universities of applied sciences in the Netherlands, Belgium, the UK and Germany has expanded the boundaries of the ecosystem.

In the ecosystem it is all about the atmosphere and the tacit culture of the people working at High Tech Campus Eindhoven and working with each other. A small example expresses this tacit cultural aspect. Cees Admiraal elaborates on a recent visit to Silicon Valley to explain the atmosphere of the ecosystem:

> . . . during one of our visits to Silicon Valley we had to visit several companies during the morning. We got a cab and started to talk to the cab driver, it was an animated conversation and we were struck by his enthusiasm on the technological environment. Here comes the important part of the story . . . The cab driver told us enthusiastically that he was interested in understanding all technological developments and was even talking to some of the start-up companies about . . . painting his cab. Painting his cab with a special solar paint, which could absorb sunlight and generate energy . . .

Ultimately the results are impressive. The mixture of a high concentration of knowledge-intensive companies, multinationals and start-ups is essential to High Tech Campus Eindhoven. There have already been a wide range of successful start-ups on High Tech Campus Eindhoven, including Shapeways (3D printing), Civolution (supplies video-content protection for Hollywood, amongst others), Liquavista (electronic ink displays, recently acquired by Samsung) and Silicon Hive (parallel processing technology, recently purchased).

The sustainability role for people-planet-profit

High Tech Campus Eindhoven envisages a role in the sustainable environment as well. The green, park-like character of the site reflects High Tech Campus Eindhoven's focus on sustainable and environmentally friendly business practice. High Tech Campus Eindhoven managed the people-planet-profit model by means of an integrated approach. This approach is driven by:

- The aim to provide good working conditions for High Tech Campus Eindhoven residents.
- Paying attention to the environment.
- Paying attention to ecology.
- Encouraging sustainable and responsible behavior on High Tech Campus Eindhoven.

Together, the companies and institutes at High Tech Campus Eindhoven make a real difference; they expand the boundaries of technology with a view to improving our quality of life.

Expanding the High Tech Campus Eindhoven model

Amongst the ambitious goals for further growth are:

- Expanding the range of locations and facilities with new accommodations.
- Attracting new high-tech companies entering the ecosystem.
- Creating complementary R&D competencies.
- Attracting investors and venture capitalists, to support the start-ups.

High Tech Campus Eindhoven, for example, wants to expand its competencies into the area of biomedical knowledge. Entering into the realm of new competencies can also result in attracting new global companies (next to e.g. Philips, Intel) to attract R&D with complementary competencies. The regional government and business community work together and share the ambition to become a strong brand for growth and employability. This cooperation is embodied in a triple helix structure of companies, knowledge institutes and the government in the wider region of Eindhoven.

The triple helix cooperation provides benefits for all parties. The business community is aware that the transition to sustainable development is attractive, making new cooperation models relevant. For High Tech Campus Eindhoven this is a cornerstone for the knowledge system to ensure a constant inflow and outflow of knowledge, resulting in profitable business.

Newtricious — Discovering the Ultimate Value of Eggs and Managing the Knowledge Chain from Agro to Nutrition

The leading question

How can a European market leader in the production and distribution of egg products transform into a knowledge enterprise in the food nutrition and life sciences segment?

The company profile

Newtricious was founded with the aim of developing a new generation of specialized nutrition that contribute to a better health and well-being. Newtricious is a Dutch life sciences company, and works in partnerships with leading scientists, innovative companies, organizations and public authorities. The roots of this company remain in the entrepreneurial spirit of the market-leading company specialized in the production and distribution of eggs.

The company's goal is to develop, jointly with other parties, a new generation of active food ingredients and products that can contribute to a better quality of life. In the past few years the firm has developed a promising pipeline and solid intellectual property (IP) rights portfolio. This portfolio entails IP in various health areas, such as obesity, metabolic syndrome, eye health, cardiovascular health and diabetes. The company is firmly positioning its knowledge in key disease and lifestyle areas.

How an agricultural firm can transform itself

The entrepreneurial CEO, Jos Nelissen, remarks: "We are inspired by Darwin. It is not the strongest of the species that survives, nor the most intelligent that survives. It is the one that is the most responsive to change . . ."

The CEO elaborates on the challenges faced in the agricultural sector. The agricultural sector is mainly engaged in production at high volumes. The companies resident in the market are primarily production driven companies. Traditionally the agricultural producers have less connection with the market and certainly not with the end user. The strategic question for many companies is what the focus of the company should be. Predominantly the focus in the sector is on scale and cost-effectiveness. The CEO envisaged that the market would be in a continuing race for scale and cost-efficiency. The consequences for certain product areas would result in end-of-product-life-cycle scenarios. Jos Nelissen explains: "If you look in the greenhouse vegetable and intensive farming sector, the companies provide similar, commodity products and there is hardly any distinctive advantage. The route to the market, is producing cheaper than your competitors . . ."

Distribution as a core competency at Globus Egg

The roots of Newtricious reside in the egg production firm Globus Egg, which was founded in 1998 and had 8% market share. The Netherlands is the world's number one exporter, distributing at large volumes. The best-performing companies in the market were those firms with distribution power and the competency to manage the value chain from production of eggs towards the retail market. Globus Egg was a trading company and able to set the standard in the market to add value to the egg trading market. The company was a first mover and is still very successful. Among their core competencies is their use of a high-quality control system and managing a demonstrable quality in the value chain. Globus Egg developed and used a revolutionary tracking and tracing system, with a methodology that even traces back to the raw materials of the feeding. Good tracing of the origins and the residues from goods and raw materials is a main topic in the current agricultural markets. Globus Egg had a very strong control over the chain management which resulted in adding value to the product.

Also in the distribution process the company introduced a process innovation. For example, they developed a new logistics system which reduced 50% percent of the logistics costs. This was, however, only a temporary competitive advantage since their smart use of stock pallet systems was soon copied by the competition.

In their quest for added value, CEO Jos Nelissen set off down another road with Globus Egg. The company was in the continuing race of scale and efficiency but the CEO decided that this focus was just not good enough:

> You are only concerned with making savings on costs . . . however you should start with the ultimate questions like: 'What is the value

of eggs? What do I actually produce for the end user? What are their end emotional benefits? Can we deliver other value from the product itself? What is the potential to adapt a product or improve a product or to make new products?'

The turning point — the quest for the added value of eggs

The company had control over their full production system for eggs. The management team gained the insights that they would not be able to grow, especially so considering the fact they had set the European standards for maximum cost-efficiency. The management team took the decision to make the step towards the consumer, a crucial step. The CEO remarks: "I knew it was not easy. What are we going to do? How can we learn and which competencies do we need? . . ." Together with some partners in the value chain they set up a foundation. Their primary goal was to get the answers to the ultimate question: "What is the ultimate added value of eggs?"

The team decided to take a roadmap to discover this value in the upcoming three years. The people involved had a mission: the ultimate quest for value, a strategic roadmap lasting for three years by a core team of six people. Their strategy (Fig. 1) was not directed towards restructuring the portfolio or finding areas for improvement and breakthroughs on the cost side. Their strategy was not to do similar activities or even better activities. Their strategy was to find a different roadmap: not merely an organizational transformation but even industrial pioneering. To extend their leadership as a company, they ultimately needed to reinvent leadership, and to reinvent leadership it had to reinvent the industry, and to reinvent the industry it had to ultimately reinvent its strategy (e.g. Hamel & Prahalad, 1994). What was needed was pioneering and discovering

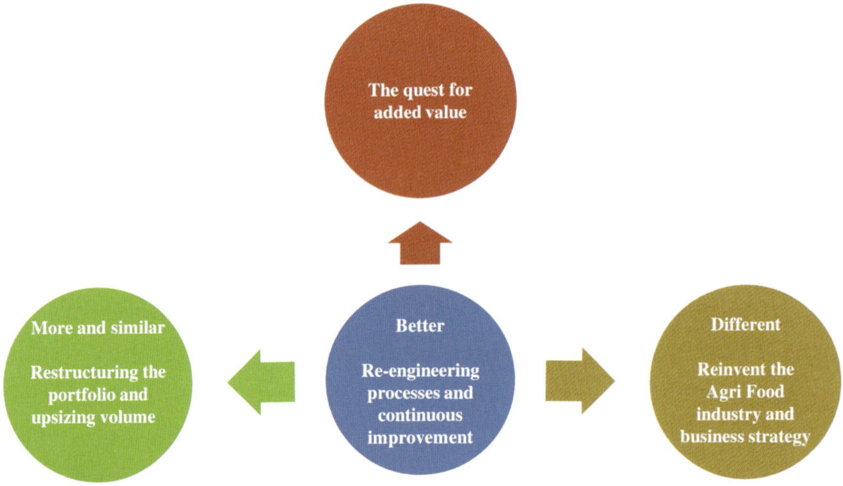

Fig. 1. The quest for value — more, better and different at Newtricious. Reproduced with permission of Newtricious.

all available options pertaining to the added value of the egg product.

The company took a structural and strategic approach, in which the end consumer was the starting point.

End-consumer research. To find the consumer insights and psychological reasonings of consumers as to why they buy, use and eat egg products.

A value chain analysis of the entire chain. The activity focussed on defining the value chain map in Europe and later a global chain analysis. In the map they discovered the routings, e.g. where eggs are produced, where they are consumed, at which amount and the numbers, including the distribution lines.

Purchasing and retail analysis. Subsequently they have set up a purchasing information and quality program, based upon the information of European purchasers of egg volumes. They interviewed all purchasers of eggs in Europe that are important. The team invested time to meet and interview the senior buyers of egg-related products of European retailers like ALDI and Albert Heijn.

Seizing the business potential — short- or long-term opportunities?

Based upon the strategic analysis, together with input from Wageningen University, there appeared to be several strategic recommendations on the potential for added value of egg products. Among the value potential appeared several options for a new market positioning:

- Value proposition directed at a rapid invasion in the market, which one could do with new packing propositions.
- Value proposition directed at a quick marketing campaign and a promotional campaign to increase retail sales volumes.

Certainly, these were all value-creating activities, which the company could start as of tomorrow and which would make it to the store shelf the day after. The good news about these propositions was the positive feasibility.

But the CEO explains: "The bottom-line conclusion appeared to be another business model direction . . . the highest added value was residing in the application of health . . ." But seizing this business potential puts high requirements on company size, new skills, high volume, capital needs etc. At that time the company was lacking competencies in the crucial areas of science, medication and healthcare.

The core team reflected and redirected to unmet needs (see Fig. 2). They approached from another angle in trying to find unexploited opportunities, which created a new value map. By looking at the value chart and asking: "Where is the highest

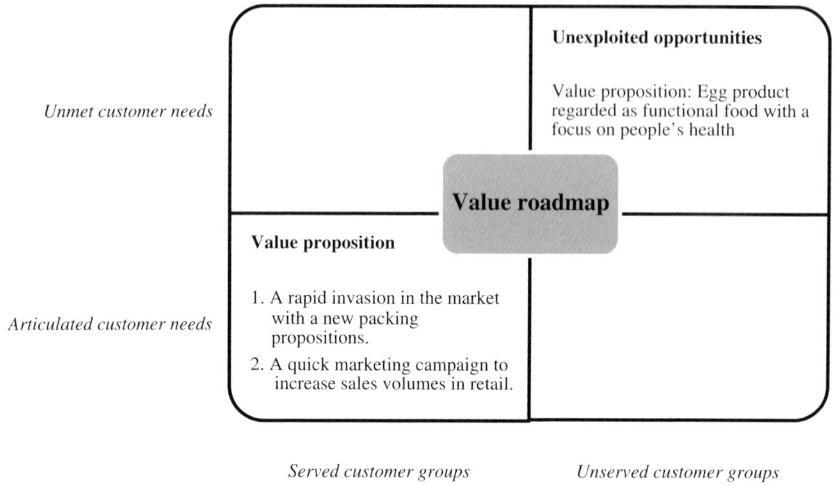

Fig. 2. Reinventing the business model: value mapping by Newtricious. Reproduced with permission of Newtricious.

added value? What takes the most time? What requires most capital? And which area entails most risk? What skills and competencies are needed to raise the organization towards the next level?" In their quest they found a destination for the value quest. The ultimate value proposition appeared to be the egg product as functional food with a focus on people's health. What must be done to ensure that the company and the industry evolves in that direction?

The golden egg insight — the nutritional value of the egg

The breakthrough in the discussion was based upon the insight that an egg incorporates all necessary nutritional ingredients for an embryo chicken to grow as it resides inside the egg. This was already supported by all kinds of scientific studies. The chicken protein of the egg has a high nutritional value. The protein also resembles the human protein. Furthermore the egg yolk includes a lot of valuable nutrients that one can use in food that promotes people's health.

The CEO was still reflecting on the business potentials and how to acquire the needed, but missing, competencies. In 2002 they set up a program with Wageningen University, joining a project of Unilever relating to functional food. The company then initiated within two months a private consortium and submitted a large European project. The first grant brought enough funding for scientific research with Wageningen University and the medical section of Groningen University. It took two years to gain evidence to extract chicken protein peptides from eggs that can have a blood-pressure-lowering effect upon humans. Together with scientists they performed a literature study on research on eggs and related substances in scientific studies. Thus, the scientific literature was screened and mapped, including what the current status of patents in the field was.

The company observed three striking conditions:

1. There was a lot of research done with impressive results.
2. There was a large volume of research that had accumulated over the past 50 years.
3. There were almost no patents.

This business insight was strengthened and confirmed from the egg chain system, because the existing companies in the sector remained traditional and production focussed.

Beyond the golden egg discovery — building up the organization on competencies

The CEO remarks upon his philosophy for innovation:

> You must assume that you do not know a lot of things. And to be ultimately successful, you have to get all these skills onboard. Well, we

> have established Newtricious on this organizing principle . . . We are actually a network company. We have a core team, surrounded by a network of layers of consultations and scientific institutions. But also a variety of sectors of specialization. In 2004 the company arrived at a landmark in time and their first patent was requested. A crucial stage for the company. Part of the management team considered this breakthrough as 'O.K. the golden egg has arrived, now we can earn.'

The CEO was thinking about all the things that had to be done in the near future.

Newtricious started to build upon the missing competencies: capital and also the skills of people who can think beyond industry boundaries. They invested in gaining knowledge and skills from pharmaceutical areas, medical biology amd protein hydrolysates. Newtricous learned from the practices of companies in other industries. The company incorporated the principles from pharmaceutical R&D models and they investigated the necessary competencies from the biotech sector. The pharmaceutical R&D model is relevant and includes a great level of creativity in any case with biotech. Newtricious invested in networking, people and appealing competencies areas. Newtricious' business model was to claim the value of eggs based upon good scientific research; this was a basic requirement from the beginning. This came to be of crucial importance as, in 2007, new legislation on healthcare was introduced.

Competency development based upon scientific evidence and research

The new legislation was an advantage for Newtricious. As of 2007 it meant that health or health-related claims on food had to be approved or registered (this is a very difficult, capital-intensive process). Clinical studies have to prove that there is scientific evidence, demonstrable effect and that it is safe. This often results in a cost-intensive trajectory for many years. This is very similar to pharmaceuticals. But for Newtricious there was an advantage: the food industry is not yet at the scientific claims level and great differences exist between European countries and market leaders in the food industry with functional food.

Newtricious started growing in 2007 and in 2008 started performing a lot of scientific studies. In these years the pharmaceutical company Organon was acquired by Schering-Plough Corporation. Later the Merck Company acquired Schering-Plough. Newtricious employed some people from this company to strengthen its pharmaceutical competencies in order to understand the human body and brain effects better. Newtricious was thus doing much research on the medical side. New knowledge was needed and developed over this period in the areas of chronic diseases to build up for this lacked competency. In 2010 the company employed several new people with a track record in the biotech.

Award-winning research with one goal — develop knowledge and secure health claims

The knowledge strategy is to develop functional foods through partnering with innovative industries and leading knowledge institutes. At the company level the team works towards securing regulatory health claims in almost all of the company's developments. The company's R&D efforts including *in vitro* research, clinical development and product development.

All this knowledge accumulation is conducted according to contemporary science and worldwide regulatory requirements.

This has resulted in several innovation awards:

- In appreciation of its innovative achievements, Newtricious was awarded the prestigious Food Valley Award in October 2008.
- Newtricious was also nominated for the SME Innovation Top 100, the Blue Tulip award, and the Fresh Top 100 in 2008, finishing high in the rankings for these awards.

A clear vision for the market — the century of health and well-being

Between 2008 and 2010 the company conducted several studies with the Maastricht University, including a marketing study. One of the actual studies was to find the market entry conditions and clues for market opportunities, for example, on bone health, cardiovascular diseases or immunity; essentially in search of all health-related areas where eggs actually have options. The company investigated in the smart routes to the market:

- They looked at trends.
- Watched "how the market develops."
- Considered the horizons for program development for the upcoming five to seven years before the time-to-market.
- Effected a solid assessment of the market to build upon trends, not hypes, and to ensure proper market entry.

For Newtricious the leading trend, still very strong, is that the current society is in a century of health and well-being. The CEO remarks:

> People are behind in the evolution of the changing society. Our body and our mind is still set to the metaphor of hunting and chasing food. Well, maybe not quite the spirit. Our environment is developed forward a 100 years and we (as people) walk behind in evolution.

> We are still tempted when we see food to hoard. And we move a lot less. Our lifestyle makes moving much less important. So, people are inclined to become fat. And that creates all kinds of problems with overweight and obesity. This causes all kinds of chronic diseases and conditions. So, in many countries there is an overweight problem of the population of 35% and of 12% in the case of young people, that is already dangerous . . .

Newtricious has evolved even further since 2010, from prevention of chronic diseases to a level of lifestyle change (to develop people's consciousness to change their lifestyle and food nutrition). Newtricious' focus is not on people who are sick. Newtricious focuses on people who are in a risk group. So, Newtricious is not focussed on treatment. Newtricious is focussed on prevention. And that's a whole different ball game. This requires a different perspective on the healthcare system in countries, for example the Netherlands, where lifestyle perspectives are still not implemented. Many healthcare systems are still in the business model: "We wait until someone is sick and diagnosed. And then we have a course of treatment." Newtricious operates in the field: "How can one identify the group that is susceptible to certain diseases?" With quick diagnosis. With early diagnosis, for example, a high-speed measurement method is needed to identify and promote awareness amongst professionals.

Mission critical — brains, cardiovascular and age-related-blindness knowledge

Over the years the strategy of Newtricious blurred somewhat, sometimes due to lack of knowledge, and sometimes due to investments in broad areas. In the meantime they structured the organization and formulated a mission. Projects must adhere to these mission-critical activities. The portfolio now ranges from cardiovascular disease to age-related blindness and the attendance for the brain disorder function. The latest research projects are focussed on obesity. Together with one of the largest obesity clinics in the Netherlands the company develops diets with increased protein products. That is a project with a short time-to-market. However, other programs take longer. This is the case with the extent of research on elderly blindness needed to develop more protein-based products. And cardiovascular disorders, the company has to work on several products, also in various consortia. The main programs use up to 80% of the R&D budget. These are all programs that have a development time between six and ten years. The financing of these programs sums up to millions (starting from scratch to getting an approval for a health claim is in the range of three to five million euros).

Organizing by collaborative innovation

The CEO explains further:

> But, we also need to know of course about the latent need of end consumers. You actually start with answering the question of the unmet needs. But it affects your whole product development and R&D process. If we have an R&D journey of three years, subject to three years by doing clinical trials, we need to be sure from the beginning. If you start with the wrong product and consumer assumptions in the beginning and you do fine tuning of the product at the end, you would have to do all clinical studies over again. So, we have to think very early in the development about the final product . . . Which substance? What flavor? What kind of powder? A drink? In effect you should know all this beforehand. To solve this problem we organize expert meetings in the field of marketing. Already in the early phase of the new product development process. Well, I think we have developed this into a core competency. It entails close teamwork. For instance, we had a strong cooperation with a corporation like Friesland Campina to collaborate on the effects of protein Hydrolysates.

Typical for the organization model of Newtricious is their collaborative thinking from the beginning. And trying to ensure that all parties join to develop such a product, and bring it to the final stage. Collaborative innovation is crucial to market an idea by a consortium from the very beginning. Newtricious negotiates with multinational companies, like Unilever or Nestlé. In the business model it is actually quite simple. Newtricious has set up their organization in order to settle for licensing or out-licensing to third parties. Sometimes Newtricious is part of a consortium, including a company with industrial scale and there is no need to license out the patent for production. It is a different discussion when joining a big producer as consortium partner. Newtricious has already gained production know-how, since they have already done various pilot projects. This gives confidence to the company for the final stage of market entry. Newtricious would then almost certainly set up a joint venture with them when going to the market.

Transition leadership — contribute to a better world

More and more topics centering upon healthcare, well-being and nutrition play an important role in people's lives. Newtricious has defined its mission to make a difference in one's personal health and well-being by creating healthy and nutritious foods. Together with scientists, Newtricious conducts research regarding the health issues of individual ingredients, which ultimately provide the knowledge to introduce convenient and healthy food to people all over the world. Newtricious' mission is to contribute to a better world, through the development of unique scientific knowledge in the field of functional foods. The company's foresight: food can play an active role in the prevention and mild treatment of chronic diseases. Central to the company's vision is a focus on improving the quality of life.

The CEO concludes: "... this is the century of finding solutions to contributing to a better world. I am 100% sure. The only question is how long it will take to move from curative to preventive solutions ..."

Chapter 5

Moving Frontiers and Solving Patients' Unmet Medical Needs — Janssen Pharmaceutical Companies of Johnson & Johnson

The leading question

How does a thought and global market leader in the development of pharmaceuticals transform its knowledge organization in search of breakthroughs in therapeutic competencies?

Everyone agrees that innovation is important, and many companies proclaim that they are assigning top business priority to innovation and customer value. In this section we shall take a closer look at Janssen Pharmaceutical companies of Johnson & Johnson, a company that is striving to become number one in therapeutic areas and to make a societal impact. It is an insightful corporate story about transforming an organization into one that thrives on customer focus, addresses unmet medical needs and partakes in collaborative innovation. First, we present the global story of Johnson & Johnson and the pharmaceutical business, as represented by the Janssen Pharmaceutical companies. Next, we examine the organization of innovation by Janssen Pharmaceutical companies. We consider the worldwide innovation strategy and its execution and investigate the campus strategy at the regional level in Benelux (Belgium, the Netherlands and Luxembourg) and Europe.

The aspiration, roots and credo of Johnson & Johnson

The Johnson & Johnson family of companies has existed for more than 125 years and is committed to caring for people. This is reflected in the Johnson & Johnson strategic framework (see Fig. 1). The commitment to caring for people, a legacy of the founders and a motivating force among its 128,000 employees, is embodied in the company credo: "Our first responsibility is to the doctors, nurses, patients, the mothers and fathers, and all who use our products." The credo, Johnson & Johnson's corporate ethical code, serves as the daily guideline for all the work done in the operating companies. By caring for one person at a time, Johnson & Johnson aspires to help billions of people live longer, healthier, happier lives.

The stock-market-listed companies' core businesses are built on this credo, which is written down in a unique set of strategic principles (see Fig. 1). The strategic principles entail four guidelines, incorporated in both the growth strategy of the companies and their organizational design:

1. Johnson & Johnson is broadly based in healthcare.
2. The company focus is on managing for the long term.
3. Johnson & Johnson operates under a decentralized management approach.
4. The company operates through a unique culture that values and fosters the development of its people.

Fig. 1. Corporate strategy of Johnson & Johnson. Reproduced with permission of Johnson & Johnson.

In today's highly competitive global marketplace, it is essential that Johnson & Johnson focuses on the four critical drivers of growth:

1. Creating value through innovation.
2. Local focus in parallel with global reach.
3. Executing business activities with excellence in everything they do.

4. Inspiring leadership with purpose among the people who carry on the Johnson & Johnson legacy.

Johnson & Johnson has three healthcare business groups: the Janssen group (like prescriptive medicines and diagnostics, or medicines in areas of neurodegenerative diseases, oncology, cardiovascular, immunology, infectious diseases), consumer products (like skin care and baby products), and medical devices and diagnostics (like hip and knee replacements, sterilization products, disposable contact lenses). All pharmaceutical activities of Johnson & Johnson are bundled together under the name "Janssen Pharmaceutical companies."

The origins of Janssen Pharmaceutical companies

Janssen Pharmaceutical companies is a part of the Johnson & Johnson corporation, one of the largest and most well-respected healthcare corporations in the world. Johnson & Johnson is active in more than 60 countries and incorporates over 250 sister companies.

Founded in 1953 by Dr. Paul Janssen, who started his own research in his father's company in Belgium, Janssen Pharmaceutica has a strong history. In 1961, it was acquired by the Johnson & Johnson corporation, becoming a knowledge leader in the healthcare domain. It has a strong level of autonomy within the Johnson & Johnson corporation. In the different countries of Europe, the company is organized to harmonize with the local healthcare systems and stakeholders. Janssen focuses on the discovery, development, production, and marketing and sales of new medicines and diagnostics. It works on providing innovative therapies for patients, doctors, and other healthcare professionals. Janssen's operating companies are responsible for the marketing and sales activities of these therapies.

Janssen encompasses three large functional groups: research & development (R&D), the supply chain and the commercial organization. In 2011 its pharmaceutical R&D expenditures were $5,136 million, equivalent to 21.1% of sales in the pharmaceutical segment of Johnson & Johnson. Pharmaceutical R&D expenditures for the year 2012 were $5,362 million, equivalent to 21.2% of sales in the pharmaceutical segment of Johnson & Johnson.

The need for a new business model — addressing unmet medical needs

Living longer, healthier and happier lives is a true statement of customer focus. In the past few years the pharmaceutical industry has faced dramatic changes in its market conditions. Due to societal changes and cost pressure, the economic viability of national healthcare systems came under attack. New regulations and societal drivers in the healthcare systems provided a stress test for the business model. Today, companies in the healthcare and pharmaceutical domain face more stakeholders and more competition and a rapidly evolving market.

This was a moment of truth for the healthcare companies and a wake-up call to question the current business model. The traditional model for pharmaceutical companies did not fit anymore, based as it was upon a long-term R&D cycle and patenting for a lengthy time period. It required rethinking the revenue model and creating a new strategy for seizing control of industry changes and creating the markets of tomorrow. Basically, new competitive realities appeared that ruptured the market boundaries, and the traditional model gradually became obsolete. For example, a competitive position based upon a "me too" strategy combined with long lead times would no longer be effective.

Janssen was keen to shift its focus to a customer-centric business model in order to create beneficial outcomes for patients in therapeutic domains. Thinking about these markets of tomorrow demands better treatment models and truly understanding the patients' medical needs and their perceptions and evolving behavior.

Among the key transformation drivers are the changing healthcare systems in the different countries in Europe. Healthcare insurance developments, new policy rules, and tighter cost control for medical care have had an impact. The life cycle and return on investment for certain medicines has substantially decreased over the past few years. These new rules of the business game were foreseen by the board of Janssen. This required the company to consolidate and turn around the R&D efforts, assess the return on investment potential (of specialties and generic medicines), and accept a shorter life cycle model for new medicines.

One of the strategic directions taken was to refocus on specific therapeutic areas. Janssen held a strong position in certain therapeutic domains, including a promising portfolio of premarket development products, patents, and go-to-market initiatives. The strategic direction included finding the answer to the question, "Are we doing the right things right?" Janssen opted to divest in certain therapeutic domains and focus on a strong set of growth areas.

This entailed withdrawing from the development of certain therapeutic areas, e.g. antimycotics. At the same time, Janssen divested in several medical areas and created a spinout strategy of their unique competencies in gastroenterology. It also changed its position in the area of oncology compounds. The company broadened its portfolio of products, knowledge and competencies in certain therapeutic areas. Addressing unmet medical needs became a theme in its growth strategy. The guidelines of this new growth strategy are:

- A patient-/customer-centric focus, addressing unmet medical needs.
- Turning the organization into a customer-oriented entity.
- Creating greater added value in patient care and the appearance of personalized medicine.
- Targeting specific stakeholder groups and therapeutic areas.
- A core competency focus on five therapeutic areas.
- Evolution of the R&D organization into smaller groups end-to-end and an organization that partakes in innovation with an open collaboration model.

Become number one in five therapeutic areas

Janssen's strategic goal for the year 2020 is ambitious: to be number one in five therapeutic areas, namely neurosciences, oncology, vaccines and infectious diseases, immunology, and cardiovascular and metabolic disorders. By 2020, Janssen aims to be the world leader in treating complex disorders for which no sufficiently efficacious treatments are yet available. Scientific excellence and innovation are combined to provide breakthroughs and answers for difficult medical challenges.

Becoming number one is an endeavor, but how can a company build a strategy and structure that will make a difference in the industry? It implies questioning and redefining the frontiers of the pharmaceutical industry and business model. Janssen's strategy is designed and directed towards a clear "go-to-market" strategy combined with the target to create more innovations in particular medical fields. But how should such a strategy be executed? This requires new operating rules in R&D activities. The senior vice president (SVP) of the Janssen open innovation campus in Belgium, Dr. Ludo Lauwers, talks about this subject:[1]

> In order to come up with innovative and differentiated products that will address unmet medical needs and in order to continuously fill the pipeline, the company needs to tap into the best science in the world, collaborate widely and review drastically the way R&D is performed. Amongst the strategic approaches taken is to invest in the model for open innovation with an entrepreneurial and open campus model, while ensuring the business operations improve their operational excellence.

The research organization in Beerse, Belgium, has been incorporated into a single global organization, together with research centers in other European countries and the US. This model is dedicated to the five core research areas: neurosciences, infectious diseases and vaccines, oncology, immunology, and cardiovascular and metabolic conditions. The focus in Belgium is mainly on research within the first three areas.

The company is developing more products and devotes a large percentage of the R&D pipeline to developing new differentiated products and adapting current products to address the unmet medical needs. At Janssen the focus is on managing for the long term. The company's leadership position is shown by numerous figures.

- On a global scale, 70% of its sales are from products that are number one or number two in global market share. Key to this long-term approach is a disciplined portfolio management, maintaining focus on specific therapeutic areas, and building a critical mass of innovation in these disease strongholds.

[1] All unreferenced quotes are taken from interviews held with the respective companies at their company headquarters during 2012 and 2013.

- Approximately two-thirds of the growth over the past ten years has come from organic growth tied to innovation, with the balance coming from licensing, partnerships and acquisitions.
- Johnson & Johnson is currently among the most successful pharmaceutical companies in launching new medicines.

The transformation journey

Over the past five years, Janssen has gradually transformed the way it operates in the business units and markets. The organization's challenge is to build upon the key values of innovation, trust, societal relevance, and healthcare impact for patients. As the managing director of the commercial organization of Janssen in Benelux, Sonja Willems, states:

> The transformation is an ongoing journey: a journey to transform the culture, invest in personal development, be aware of the change resistance in people and provide a positive culture for change... How can we ensure that we shall be successful? Engage our people in the strategic thinking and direction we want to take, take them along on the journey and if possible 'chunk it:' reduce the transformation process to small, manageable steps.

At the same time several organizational conditions were created to improve the organizational performance. First of all, the company built up capabilities for operational excellence. Organizational processes were aligned and drivers for cost reductions implemented. In the transformation journey the company strengthened its ability to ensure that operating expenses remain under control. Furthermore, the company's leading role was consolidated as it claimed more responsibility in managing the healthcare network. This was achieved by strengthening the organizational network linkages. Janssen put its efforts into a dialogue with stakeholders in the government, healthcare professionals, and patients to campaign for a more effective system. The cultural heritage of Janssen was further enabled and directed towards a philosophy of entrepreneurship with a focus on the people factor — investing in human capital. During this transformation journey, Janssen invested in its personnel, dedicating itself to its role as a trusted partner in the healthcare system, while continuing to develop new competencies in the therapeutic areas. This is consistent with the Janssen philosophy of making a societal impact.

Make a societal impact and meet unmet medical needs

Johnson & Johnson's corporate accountability stretches across many fields, including helping society with access to medicine. The annual Access to Medicine Index 2012 (see Fig. 2) positions Johnson & Johnson as a rising star and gives it second place in the ranking (rated ninth in 2010). What does the access to Access to Medicine Index stand for? Millions of people in the world have no access to medicine. The Index is an independent ranking and gives insight into what the pharmaceutical industry is doing to improve this situation. It ranks pharmaceutical companies' efforts to improve access to medicine in developing countries. Funded by the Bill & Melinda Gates Foundation and the UK and Dutch governments, the Index has been published every two years since 2008 (www.accesstomedicineindex.org). Improvements can take place in the areas of availability, accessibility of medicine management or affordability. But also the company's conduct of relationships with policymakers, competitors, customers and the general public on health matters. And of course the R&D efforts that are aimed at producing relevant products.

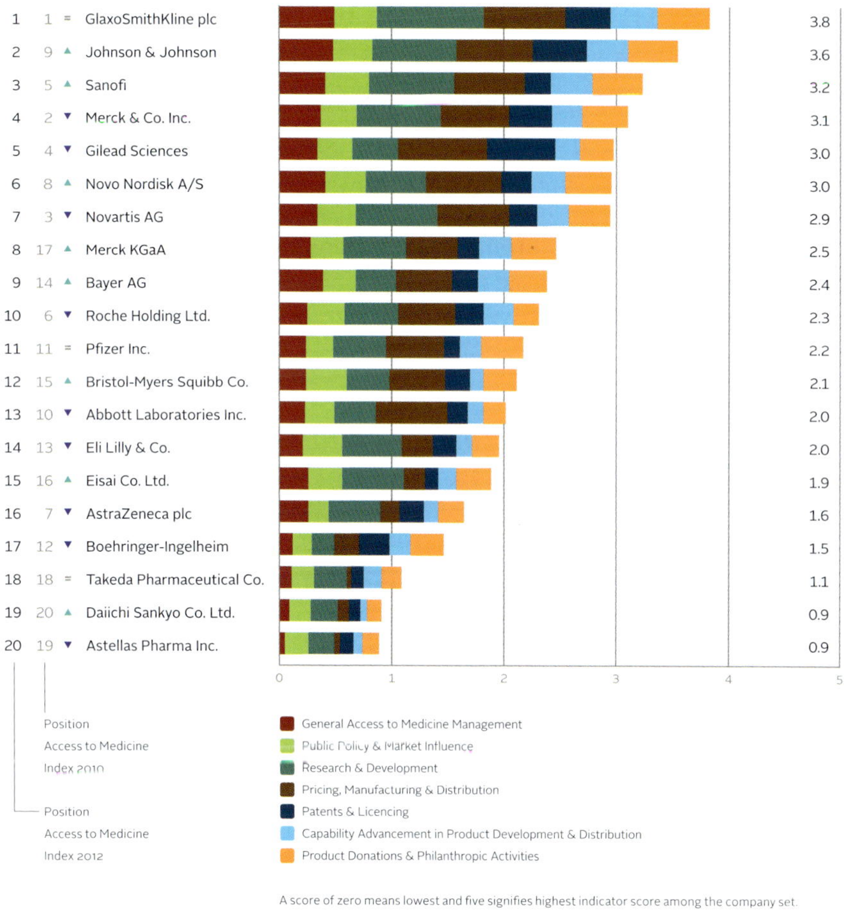

Fig. 2. The Access to Medicine Index 2012 — overall ranking. Published with permission, source: The Access to Medicine Index 2012, http://www.accesstomedicineindex.org/sites/www.accesstomedicineindex.org/files/ 2012-access-to-me dicine-index-clickable.pdf.

The Janssen group of pharmaceutical companies is constantly investing in the availability of medication to all nations and people on the planet. Among the range of examples is the investment in the fight against tuberculosis (TB). The entirely unique compound for combating multi-drug-resistant tuberculosis (MDR-TB) developed by Janssen is particularly relevant for many African countries. Janssen can make a real difference in fighting MDR-TB and has further developed its expertise in this area, primarily for the benefit of society's health. The managing director, Sonja Willems, states:

> At Janssen, the quest is in understanding unmet needs, whilst knowing what you are doing and researching, and for whom, and during this innovation process making the right choices (doing the right things right).

The power of the lateral organization of Janssen Pharmaceutical companies

The Janssen group of companies has introduced the phenomenon of disease strongholds to align its R&D and business units. To be successful with this strategy, it is important that each of the participating entities puts a great deal of energy into the growth perspectives. But organizational design is a key attribute to make the strategy work. Characteristic of Janssen's organization are the collaborative innovation functions and the decentralized market units with profit–loss responsibility for their regions. Currently, the organization of the European markets features local commercial business entities. The European R&D activity is centralized and concentrated in Belgium, established at the open innovation campus at Beerse. The European markets are split into:

- The main markets (e.g. Germany, Spain).
- The mid-size markets (e.g. Benelux, Switzerland).
- The emerging markets (e.g. Turkey, Russia).

Each country organization within the regional structure is responsible for making a profit, with its own functions of sales, marketing, medical affairs, disease management, health economics and market access, public affairs, finance, HR, etc. Janssen introduced several lateral organization structures (between the R&D and market units) in order to realize a better return on their innovation investments, thereby taking advantage of synergy instead of duplicating research and development efforts. This organization design is also directed at creating cross-lateral linkages. Typical examples of these cross-linkages are:

- The Janssen campus office at the Janssen campus in Belgium, which enables and facilitates innovation for sustainable future healthcare, supporting all the functional groups present on the Belgium campus.
- Alignment of Janssen's supply chain function, for chemical manufacturing, with Janssen commercial, for the commercial markets of e.g. EMEA (Europe, the Middle East and Africa) and Benelux.
- Close connection with the customer's needs. For example, the use of "value teams" in Germany to search for new value propositions, based upon patients' needs.

By means of such organizational designs, the company constitutes a lateral organization and unique collection of expertise and capabilities. This helps to unite the innovation activities. In a sense, the lateral thinking of the organization is empowered and helps to find therapeutic solutions for significant unmet medical needs.

Mobilizing entrepreneurship, getting engaged with consumers

Idea generation is not the sole domain of R&D or of the innovation heavyweight project team. Janssen is committed to mobilizing idea generation throughout the organization, which has proved to be conducive to success. In a sense, the management is decentralizing innovation and passing responsibility to the individual. Everyone can have a great idea, and everyone is supported in the generation of these ideas. In fact, more ideas make a better company. There is a potential for breakthrough ideas to occur through serendipity: in the EMEA countries, for example, Janssen supports the wide idea initiative by means of an innovation funnel. The process is essentially a spark for corporate entrepreneurship. The management focuses on improving the talents and competencies of the human capital factor in the organization. The funnel's function exclusively rewards project ideas which are not already included in the regular business. Employees are encouraged to search for new ideas that are thought-provoking and relevant to Janssen's ambitions. All employees in the region can submit an innovative idea to the innovation funnel, thus giving the organization new impetus in its transformation into a learning organization. Two examples can be used to demonstrate the success of this way of working. Ideas from the employees can have a simple, yet highly effective impact on increasing engagement with the consumers and gaining new insights into certain disease areas.

- Collaboration with an engaged generation — The practice of the "Young Lions Parliament." This idea began with a reflection of the German Bundestag and young people. There is a youth version of the Bundestag, Junior Bundestag, which operates in the same way. Janssen installed a "Young Lions Parliament" of 150 young people and debates major topics on health and lifestyle on a regular basis.
- Collaboration — The practice of the "Avatar" teams: Several teams of multidisciplinary functions from Janssen were given

an assignment to learn from companies in other industries. The teams gained new insights on market trends and company tactics, which inspired the people from Janssen to look at their own business from a different angle.

Innovation — in search of breakthroughs — noblesse oblige

The roots of the company go back to the founding days of Dr. Paul Janssen. This anchor role is based on finding breakthrough innovations in areas of high-impact diseases. The track record of breakthroughs includes medicines on schizophrenia, morphine for heart surgery, and anti-fungal infection medications (for humans and animals). All innovations belong to the list of pharmaceutical breakthroughs that were primarily driven by the motivation to find medical solutions to complex diseases. This attitude is not dominated by short-term goals, but by enduring commitment to innovation, although with the necessary sense of urgency. But this takes time. "You cannot boil the ocean overnight," says the SVP of the Janssen campus in Belgium, Dr. Ludo Lauwers, as he metaphorically stresses the importance of timelines in the transformation. The Janssen roots are a guideline and determine the pace and rhythm for today's organization in its search for innovation. Janssen is committed to creating the future of healthcare. The management has identified ten major trends impacting that future: the aging population, customization, sustainability, the changing competition, therapy adherence, upcoming intelligent materials and technologies, prevention, product authenticity and safety, communication and networks everywhere, and ease of use and comfort. Given these major trends, Janssen is actively developing solutions in the therapeutic areas of focus. This is characterized by five innovation rules, which describe "the way we operate around here:"

- Innovation rule #1: unmet medical needs.
- Innovation rule #2: focus on solutions for the five therapeutic areas.
- Innovation rule #3: collaborative innovation — "the world is our lab."
- Innovation rule #4: core competency and team focus on disease strongholds.
- Innovation rule #5: getting proof of concept.

Innovation rule #1 — unmet medical needs

The first and most important driver is the search for unmet medical needs and a patient- and customer-centric approach. This is best described by the slogan "the patients are waiting;" a unique philosophy rooted in the past breakthrough innovations of Janssen Pharmaceutical companies, as well as Johnson & Johnson's history. It implies the search for radical innovations instead of new application areas and "me too" products, which are a better copy of existing medical products. This puts strong demands on the organization and operating procedure in the innovation unit of Janssen.

This customer-centric approach is operational in several ways. It increases insights in the health situation and the real-life environment of patients (including the social, economic and governmental). This knowledge is fed back into the product development process in order to create, design and deliver customer-centric solutions that will make a difference.

Predictive informatics and modeling are also used to enable the analysis and recognition of trends and patterns in data sets. This allows the company to take better decisions early on in the product development process. It helps to find therapeutic solutions that resolve the real customers' needs.

Innovation rule # 2 — focus on solutions for the five therapeutic areas

The healthcare solutions address some of the world's most significant unmet medical needs. The efforts to discover medicines that treat unmet medical needs focus primarily on those disease areas for which no effective treatments are yet available. Janssen decided to invest in five clearly defined therapeutic areas. They are the knowledge domains in which Janssen can develop new products which meet the time-to-market needs of the innovation pipeline. The five therapeutic research areas are:

1. Neurosciences.
2. Oncology.
3. Vaccines and infectious diseases.
4. Immunology.
5. Cardiovascular and metabolic disorders.

These therapeutic areas provide Janssen with growth perspectives and the ability to add value to society and the healthcare of people.

Innovation rule #3 — collaborative innovation — "the world is our lab"

A third rule for innovation is as follows: "to solve the complex puzzle implies finding knowledge and combining knowledge inside and outside the company." The consequence of this perspective is that Johnson & Johnson particularly believes in what is known as "collaborative innovation."

Janssen invested in strategic alliances to build up, step by step, the role of trusted partner in the healthcare system.

Strategic initiatives that Janssen Benelux has started recently include patient care in the neurosciences stronghold and in schizophrenia.

- The PsyMate® cooperation. PsyMate® is a purpose-made device that facilitates the monitoring of daily life experience and patient behavior. Maastricht University developed PsyMate® and is the owner of this device. It is used to apply momentary assessment technology to mental health practice. It can be programmed to generate beeps at unpredictable moments of the day, reminding participants to use a touch screen to fill out small questionnaires on current mood state, social context and day-to-day activities.
- Joint research with the Trimbos Institute — "Bridging the gap" (http:// www.bridging-the-gap.nl/). The Trimbos Institute investigates the subjective quality of life of young people with a psychosis. The aim of the research is to improve their quality of life and levels of education.

The managing director of the commercial organization of Janssen in the mid-size markets region in EMEA, Kris Sterkens, provides a recent example:

> Propositions for cost savings in therapeutic domains are of incredible importance to us. Janssen has started to work with performance contracts in the domain of psychiatry. Janssen Germany took part in a tender for patient care in psychiatry in Germany. Their proposition was directed at a 360° patient care cycle in combination with searching for cost reductions in the treatment process.

Janssen was selected through a tender process to take over the integrated care management of the schizophrenic patients of the largest health insurer in Germany (AOK) for the Lower Saxony region. This is an exemplary case emphasizing Janssen's efforts to cooperate with external stakeholders to deliver better patient care.

Innovation rule #4 — Core competency and team focus on disease strongholds

The Janssen R&D organization specifically targets five therapeutic areas, as managed by heavyweight teams with a mission-critical mandate (Clark & Wheelwright, 1993). The SVP of Janssen campus in Belgium, Dr. Ludo Lauwers, emphasizes the role of these teams as a crucial ingredient to reap the returns of R&D.

The heavyweight project team in action

Let us look at the example of the heavyweight team for Alzheimer's disease. A scientific leader and a commercial leader co-chair the knowledge development of this disease stronghold. They are responsible for a team of approximately five to six key scientists, who have a mandate to search for solutions in this therapeutic area. They attempt to add to the existing knowledge on protein, the technology of imaging to detect protein, and the expertise in neurosciences and neuro-imaging. They are tasked with making joint collaboration agreements with imaging technology providers like General Electric and Siemens. In this example, it is critical to absorb knowledge on neuro-imaging in order to enable early diagnostics about the disease and its pattern of growth.

The competency imperative goes into even more detail: for each of the five therapeutic areas, there are more specific focus areas, called the disease area strongholds. For example, in the therapeutic area of infections, one of the strongholds is hepatitis C. For oncology, these strongholds are leukemia, prostate cancer and lung cancer. The mission is to obtain knowledge and build capabilities to find cures for these specific diseases. The determination of which needs constitute strongholds is primarily based upon the company's belief that these areas are the unmet medical needs.

Innovation rule #5 — getting proof of concept

The teams need to thrive and have the impetus to get breakthroughs. To build upon the competencies and solve the unmet medical needs, the teams responsible for the development of a therapeutic area are primarily driven by one goal: getting a proof of concept. They are endorsed with several key performance indicators such as:

- Targets for the number of compounds and the degree to which they are taken to the stage of proof of concept.
- The number of partners involved in finding the breakthroughs.
- The type of dosage (new ways of applying the medication, e.g. intravenously or oral dosage).

These teams also keep pace with new technologies like RFID (radiofrequency identification) technology and apps for support services and to keep track of the global ten trends in the changing healthcare landscape. New products are designed like new knee prostheses with built-in sensors. Also, opportunities arise from information technology and 3D printing electronics. These promising new technologies are important to Johnson & Johnson, and have led to partnering in a consortium network.

Innovation heartbeat — the Johnson & Johnson and Janssen strategy for collaborative innovation

The innovation strategy realization of Johnson & Johnson and Janssen encompasses several functions and roles. A recent evolution is the effort in open innovation to encourage aligned activities and organize across sectors. The three business groups of Johnson & Johnson, e.g. consumer products, medical devices and diagnostics, and Janssen group, increasingly collaborate and explore the innovation opportunities in the outside world.

The Johnson & Johnson development corporation provides venture capital for investment in external opportunities that are aligned with the overall business strategy of Johnson & Johnson. The Johnson & Johnson innovation centers have a science discovery role. They are the primary scouts to build relationships with start-ups, academic institutes and all other stakeholders involved in health care. The innovations centers' role is to discover and explore the best early-stage science in the external world and to close early-stage deals. There are four innovation centers, established in San Francisco, Boston, London and Shanghai. They are geographically distributed so that each center has full responsibility for its region.

A special function was created within the Janssen group, called Janssen healthcare innovation. Its task is specifically to explore and develop products and services that seek to transform the consumer healthcare experience.

A recent new step in the Janssen innovation strategy is the creation of Janssen labs, a "no strings attached" incubator at the Janssen R&D San Diego campus on the US West Coast.

At the regional level in Benelux and Europe, the Janssen campus in Belgium plays a pivotal role in facilitating open innovation for a sustainable healthcare future.

Janssen campus, Belgium, center of excellence

The Janssen campus in Belgium operates like a center of excellence, integrating the R&D, supply chain, commercial and supporting functions within the worldwide group of Janssen Pharmaceutical companies. It comprises legal entities and sites

Fig. 3. Janssen campus, Belgium — mission, vision and strategic goals for collaborative innovation. Reproduced with permission of Johnson & Johnson.

in Beerse, Geel, Olen and Merksem in Belgium, employing approximately 4,300 highly qualified professionals who are passionate about healthcare. As a derivative of its own mission (care for patients) and vision, three strategic goals are pursued (see Fig. 3):

1. Build an entrepreneurial community.
2. Focus on high value-added activities.
3. Make the transition to an open innovation model.

A key success factor for the open model is that Janssen's global and supporting functions are engaged in a joint strategy to take full advantage of the proximity, the knowledge density and the economies of scale.

The campus model encompasses several innovation functions like venturing, business development and stimulating entrepreneurship.

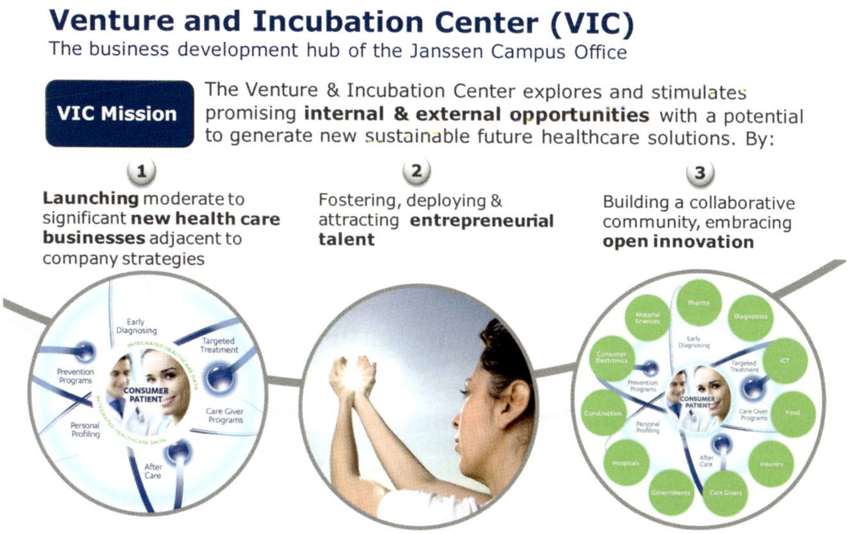

Fig. 4. The VIC. Reproduced with permission of Johnson & Johnson.

The venture and incubation center (VIC) boosts business development

A crucial part of the campus strategy incorporates a business development hub (see Fig. 4). In this strategy, the VIC mission is to explore and stimulate promising internal and external opportunities with the potential to generate new sustainable healthcare solutions. It tries to achieve this with three aligned activities.

1. Launch moderate-to-significant new healthcare businesses (adjacent to the company strategy).
2. Foster, deploy and attract entrepreneurial talent.
3. Build a collaborative community, embracing open innovation.

The VIC's role is of significant importance as it fosters knowledge development and guides the entrepreneurs towards viable business results. Its approach focuses on two stages in particular:

the business incubation stage and the venture acceleration stage. During both stages the VIC's role is to support the health-care business in its growth in four critical venture dimensions: the solution dimension, the commercial dimension, the finance dimension and the people dimension. Its activities include:

- Training and coaching idea champions in critical venture dimensions.
- Connecting to required competencies for faster implementation.
- Incubating business opportunities in a protected environment.
- Accelerating business ventures for rapid market growth.
- Guiding entrepreneurial teams in the exit phase after incubation or acceleration.

The campus model — stimulating entrepreneurship

The entrepreneurial bootcamp (see Fig. 5) is the business development action learning program of the VIC. This program is executed in close cooperation with the Vlerick Business School. The program is directed at new business opportunities (NBOs). The NBOs entail new revenue-generating products, services, or business models in markets with significant potential. They have to fit into the long-term global Janssen strategy to become a transformational medical innovator. The bootcamp approach is set up as six sequential activities:

1. Coming up with an innovative idea to be submitted to the VIC.
2. A pitch to convince the VIC jury of the idea's potential.
3. Composing a multidisciplinary bootcamp team, which involves all necessary competencies from R&D, market access, supply chain, finance, regulatory and medical affairs, IT, etc.

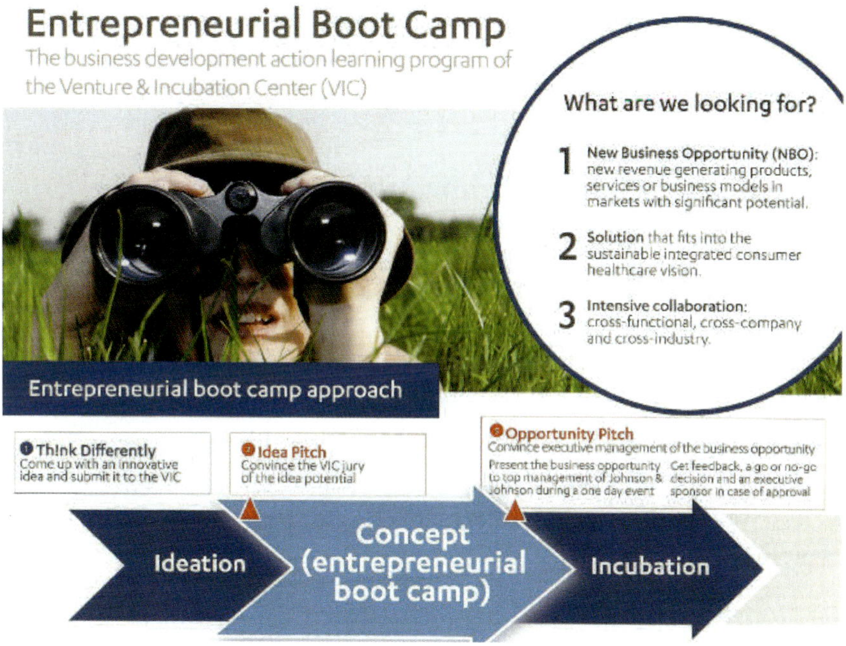

Fig. 5. The role of entrepreneurship in the Janssen campus, Belgium collaborative innovation model. Reproduced with permission of Johnson & Johnson.

4. A concept development phase: during the bootcamp period, the idea is developed by the multidisciplinary team into a solid business opportunity. This stage delivers a compelling, value-creating, business opportunity plan.
5. A pitch to convince a jury of executive management members of the business opportunity. This jury takes a decision (go/no go, feedback into regular business, separate incubation) and allocates an executive sponsor in case of approval.
6. The incubating stage starts (see the earlier VIC model): a detailed business plan is created, internal and/or external funding is actively pursued, and the solution development begins.

Among the examples of viable business ideas to arise from this bootcamp is a serious game for the ADHD patient population: Plan-it Commander.

The campus model — innovation is collaboration

The Janssen campus in Belgium has built the collaborative innovation model upon critical success factors. These factors include:

- Proximity of R&D activities.
- Building trusting and enduring relationships.
- Ensuring confidentiality.
- Keeping a clear sense of the intellectual property rights in the early stages of innovation.

The SVP, Dr. Ludo Lauwers, of the Janssen campus in Belgium states that "the way we operate around here can be described as collaborative innovation, which actually means sharing knowledge, risks and funding." This is relevant for innovation projects with a time span of four months to 14 years. Collaboration is about sharing; in particular, sharing risk and, eventually, the profits.

The Management Challenges for Tomorrow

Towards an engaged organization

Transformation is a journey which never stops, as stated by the managing director of the commercial organization of Janssen in Benelux, Sonja Willems. In this respect, Janssen's culture is moving further towards becoming an engaged organization. Janssen has set targets to keep its ambitions on track for the year 2020. Amongst the key performance indicators is the net promoter score, which is an indication of the added value you deliver for your customers and your internal people. For each of the five therapeutic areas identified by Janssen, the net promoter score is measured, monitored, and benchmarked externally in the sector to reach the number one ranking. Other key performance indicators are directed at the operating expenses and the growth targets of the number of treated patients on a yearly basis. The employee engagement is measured constantly in the credo survey, which includes a question similar to the net promoter score. The ultimate question is: how likely is it that you would recommend the company to a friend or colleague? A total of 91% of the people working at Janssen were indicated as employee promoters, indicating their engagement and enthusiasm.

Engaged leadership program

There is an important role for management and leadership in building a trustworthy image as a company. Leadership guidelines for all of Johnson & Johnson's leaders prescribe that each manager and director spend a certain amount of time in the field, in dialogue with the other healthcare stakeholders. The managers are in close contact with the clinical stakeholders in hospitals and treatment institutions, and with the government and budget stakeholders. The new patient dynamics urge the managers to be client oriented and to have an external view as they learn from others' best practices and search for the outcomes that matter to patients and their treating physicians. As the managing director, Sonja Willems, argues, "we need to become outcome improvers . . . find solutions in medication administration instead of just providing the pill." At Johnson & Johnson, the credo and aspiration drives the company to create innovations that have a significant impact on human health and well-being.

This frames their role as professionals in a larger purpose and puts a significant responsibility on each person, manager and leader. The company fosters great leadership through strong talent development programs, offering leadership opportunities around the world in various business sectors. This is where the commercial interests and the sense of social responsibility intersect.

The people factor in the lateral organization

Human resources management aims to facilitate the horizontal career development of the knowledge workers. This is an important tool for the company to develop competencies throughout the organization.

- Training on the job: a relevant tool in rapidly developing people's expertise through fast-tracking experiences in very diverse jobs.
- Leadership and personal development: the company creates an atmosphere of "safe havens" to give people the ability to grow through learning-by-doing, without being afraid of making mistakes on the way. It provides room for learning, allowing employees to take responsibility, and motivating them to go one step further to show they can make a real difference.
- Horizontal career paths: this is an important tool for strengthening the lateral linkages and creating synergy between the markets, functions, business lines, and therapeutic areas.
- Recruitment: acquiring new employees who are ready to make a change. Leverage people's capabilities by linking current employees with new employees originating from hospitals, insurance companies, and the fast-moving consumer goods industry.

A mindset change and the ability for organization learning

From a business perspective, the change processes are remarkable: recent changes in the business affected the core competencies of the organization. A true managerial challenge lies in ensuring the knowledge systems of the company work at an organization level and an individual level. With respect to the changing circumstances, one needs to take into account the employees' perspectives because the credo is of crucial importance to the organization. A deep commitment of the employees to redirecting the firm's focus is essential for the success of the growth path of Janssen. This has been further strengthened by the changing mindset and attitude of the people from operations, commerce and R&D over recent years. The SVP of the Janssen campus in Belgium says "innovation and collaboration are especially a mindset change." Campus collaboration is operational inside the company, along with a supporting human resources management (HRM) policy, and has a significant impact. The science employees have the opportunity to be exposed to other ideas, share their preliminary thoughts and research results, and become conscious about the added value of sharing and collaborating.

A key aim for the organization's learning and absorptive capacity is to ensure that good practices and lessons learned about failures are actually shared within the large corporation. This requires an orchestration role, taken on primarily by the innovation campus model. The group of companies has already facilitated the collaboration function throughout the innovation process, but the learning ability goes one step further.

The management of Janssen faces the challenge of meeting the knowledge conditions of the next generation of employees.

These knowledge conditions range from the work–life balance to the increased pace of switching between careers and functions. Therefore, the company HRM guidelines are specifically tailored to the learning periods of employment in a job and enabling job rotation on a more frequent basis.

Leading in the Pharmaceutical Industry

The fundamental conclusion is that Janssen has managed a consistent innovation path in the turbulent, changing environment of the pharmaceutical industry. It effectively transformed its knowledge organization. The strategy of "doing the right things right" exemplifies the roadmap of Janssen. Its business model was questioned to ensure proper management of the business in a changing society. The managerial choices taken and their impact upon the main business growth areas reflect Janssen's long-term commitment. The lateral organization, open innovation model and decentralized management approach are based on the belief that innovation will take place close to patients' and customers' unmet medical needs. This philosophy seems to be critical to the expansion and growth of the company.

The company has consistently built upon the heritage of Dr. Paul Janssen and incorporated the innovation genes to transform into a new business model guided by innovation. Following five striking innovation rules, the company is ready to become number one in the therapeutic areas. Insights show us the power of transforming people, processes and the organization. The strategy is expanding and thrives on customer focus, addressing unmet medical needs, therapeutic core competencies and collaborative innovation. This is not about creating a sense of urgency in restructuring medical domains but a true commitment to moving frontiers.

Janssen Pharmaceutical companies is proving to be a thought leader in its industry and a knowledge enterprise. Their company roadmap provides evidence of leveraging upon its credo: "Our first responsibility is to the doctors, nurses, patients, the mothers and fathers, and all who use our products."

Chapter 6

Innovation Strategies for the Knowledge Enterprise

Hedging, programming, streamlining, collaborative innovation, power teams and customer engagement

This chapter describes the major trends in the strategy and management of innovation. Among the major trends are: teamwork, collaborative innovation and new management policies to invest in business development and venturing. In order to safeguard, defend and develop a leading position, boundaries, including organizational boundaries, must be stretched continuously. For the knowledge enterprise, the control of innovation processes is of special relevance. This chapter compares the market leaders presented in the previous chapters from that perspective. A typology of innovation strategies, e.g. the management policy and management systems, will provide the points of reference over time. Several innovation strategies like hedging, programming, streamlining and open innovation are viewed in this approach as developmental stages of the organization system. The lessons learned and corporate stories from the companies show some remarkable answers to the "how" question of open innovation, the power of teams and customer engagement.

There is a new wind blowing throughout the innovation landscape. This gale comes in the form of a new, dominant perspective for innovation: customer engagement to create an impact in people's lives and, even more, contribute to having a positive impact upon societal needs, and the health and well-being of people. Growth and financial objectives focus more and more on creating new markets, and scouting emerging trends and business areas. As a consequence innovation has shifted towards a deeper understanding of the end customer in the value chain. Scenario analysis, customer engagement and solving unmet customer needs are new domains in innovation management.

Customer Engagement — Innovation is Primarily Driven by Customer Needs

This customer-centric approach reveals a paradigm shift away from technological thinking and towards a needs-oriented R&D. In this needs-oriented approach, these companies have one theme in common: contributing to a better world. Similar is Janssen Pharmaceutical companies' quest for meeting unmet medical needs and their efforts to ensure a higher access to medicine. Companies also aim at customer and societal engagement, and people's healthcare, well-being and nutrition are cornerstones in the strategy and growth of the core business. Newtricious, for example, has defined a strategy with which to make a difference to people's health and well-being, and concentrate their business in the areas of food nutrition and life sciences.

Open Innovation — A Next Level of New Business Development Appears

Collaborative innovation is more than a trend and is here to stay in the business landscape. New collaborative approaches appear, such as open campus models, open innovation partnerships and explicit venturing models, to seize emerging technologies. Firms are once again investing in the organization to ensure internal and external collaboration and gain from knowledge synergy.

An upcoming phenomenon for all the companies is the strategic insight of "getting more things done by cooperating inside and outside the company." Even the classical thinking of the "not-invented-here" syndrome disappears.

It puts new requirements on the old credo: getting cash from innovation. In this respect we observe a steady appearance of the venturing role in innovation, which is an innovation function attached at the corporate enterprise level and provides guidance to innovative business ideas and (start up) ventures. Ventures outside the company are spotted, screened and taken over, and sometimes spinouts appear which accelerate the business venture for rapid market growth. Essentially it is the function to connect required competencies internally to external, new competencies and to ensure a faster time-to-market of ideas, products or technologies.

Innovation Effectiveness — The Lateral Organization is the Effective Model

Organizing cross-lateral linkages inside and outside the organization has proven successful in seizing the benefits for knowledge development activities. The art of lateral thinking and the use of lateral organization to ensure knowledge flows has been mastered by the companies considered in this book. Heavyweight project teams, venture teams, scenario planning, innovation councils, and strategic, science and R&D platforms are operational in the company structures. But streamlining raises the question of how to connect with the customer. Most companies have preserved a hybrid structure for innovation throughout the years.

Connect to the Customer — Streamlining the R&D Function

Streamlining the innovation process is still a dominant trend for R&D. Streamlining has become a steady organizational practice, and nobody is willing to go back into time.

Many companies have further decentralized their R&D efforts, to ensure a close market connection. Furthermore companies have implemented cross-organizational structures to align short-term and long-term R&D objectives. Global firms have even implemented different customer advocacy techniques and installed organizational entities to connect with customers.

- Procter & Gamble uses *everyday family life observation*, which is a method with which to gain deeper understanding of their customers. The company sends video crews and TV cameras into households around the world to capture daily routines.
- At LEGO it is all about customer centricity. LEGO rejuvenated the brand with innovation processes like LEGO Factory, crowd sourcing like the LEGO Design byME contentest, and by inviting customers to join the development team with Mindstorms.
- Cisco Systems uses *customer success engineer teams*. These teams are centralized groups that diagnose root causes of

complex customer problems and implement solutions across the business.

- Microsoft has designed an organization-wide management system to get connected. Throughout the organization a customer and partner satisfaction index provides a holistic view of the business health and trigger specific corrective actions towards customers and partners, when necessary.
- The global toy and juvenile products retailer Toys Я Us has created a *customer champion director*. The customer champion director is responsible for advocating the voice of the customer throughout the organization.

Understanding customer needs is easier said than done. Listening to customers can provide room for product improvements, better processes and more satisfied customers. The new businesses we observed in Chapters 3, 4 and 5 range from incremental to industry game changing. Some innovations simply enhance the current business and core competencies. They are more or less sustaining innovations or "adjacent" business innovations (Nagji & Tuff, 2012). But many others are of a different nature and become more disruptive, or even transformational. Business innovations on material and life sciences are transformational because they develop new products, new processes and knowledge assets. The nutritious value of eggs (Newtricious), findings solutions for Alzheimer's disease (Janssen Pharmaceutical companies) and biomedical research (DSM) create new markets and fulfill unmet customer needs. It is about developing breakthroughs and inventing solutions for emerging markets

Moving industry frontiers requires thorough investigation of the adjacent markets, technologies and product solutions. The step towards breakthroughs is dominated by the strategy of R&D. The percentages of sales spent on R&D is an indicator of this road to crossing industry boundaries. The importance of exploring scientific knowledge over the years also indicates this search. It is a matter of gaining strategic foresight and deep insights into new technologies. It is also about the ability to act, the ability to make money, and the ability to get returns from balancing of investments and divestments in the current market portfolio. Having such an organizational process presumes the ability for scouting emerging and sustainable growth areas. An enduring commitment and a long-term perspective eventually leads to a transformation of core competencies.

These developments force the companies to deal with paradoxes in their organization. What is the best way of organizing the company process to get the returns from innovation?

Innovation Strategies as Points of Identification

When comparing organizations we often tend to take random moments in time — the snapshots — as the point of departure. We try to read a successful formula from the differences we observe at moments X and Y. In fact, this is the principle of benchmarking. The risk of this approach has been documented in detail by Collins (2001), Peters and Waterman (1982) and Stacey (1996: p. 207). Peters and Waterman found eight common themes which they argued were responsible for the success of corporations. The eight themes are:

1. A bias for action, active decision making — "getting on with it." This facilitates quick decision making and problem solving, and tends to avoid bureaucratic control.
2. Close to the customer. Learning from the people served by the business.
3. Autonomy and entrepreneurship. Fostering innovation and nurturing "champions."

4. Productivity through people. Treating rank-and-file employees as a source of quality.
5. Hands-on, value-driven management philosophy that guides everyday practice, accompanied by management showing its commitment.
6. Stick to the knitting. That is stay with the business that you know.
7. Simple form, lean staff, since some of the best companies have minimal HQ staff.
8. Simultaneous loose–tight properties. This implies autonomy in shop floor activities at the same time as centralized values.

Several years after the studies had been carried out, the majority of the excellent firms disappeared from the top of the lists of most successful companies. While some of the firms returned to the top later, others became stuck in the middle. Snapshots don't show movement. Frontrunners that fall back, or average firms that are coming ahead, cannot be distinguished by just looking at moments. More important than the snapshot is the story the firms have to tell.

The company story shows the road the firm left behind, where they came from and tells us what problems and challenges they faced. And of course what steps were taken and the consequences of these steps. That is how we look at the case studies and the companies, and we will try to recognize patterns, contrasts and parallels. Beacons are a familiar means to determine one's position at sea. Similar points of identification or recognition are also relevant to the analysis of business development. For the knowledge enterprise, it is particularly relevant how the firms have given shape to the management of their knowledge development and innovation processes. At the basis of each form of process management is a specific explicit or implicit organizational logic.

Organizational studies have revealed (Collins, 2011; Cooper, 1994; den Hertog & Huizenga, 2000; Huizenga, 2004; Roussel *et al.*, 1991; Shapiro, 2013) that fixed patterns can be identified in the way in which these forms (or "regimes") of process management follow one another. Insight into that change in an organization's management systems provides reference points with which to determine a firm's current position and to chart the future course. This insight offers a framework for interpretation of one's actions. The analysis of the case studies presented will make use of the typology based on a track record of United Nations University | MERIT studies (den Hertog & Huizenga, 2000; Huizenga, 2004) into innovation processes.

Looking at the transformation horizon of the leading companies, we can identify four organizational phases (hedging, programming, streamlining and collaboration). Each phase is characterized by a specific innovation strategy, which determines the way in which priorities are identified, funding is settled, the work is divided, and progress is planned and controlled. The four phases are preceded in a historical sense by a pioneering phase, both for the ventures and the older firms, in which the lab, close to the factory, had a kind of "breakthrough function." Nowadays the large diversified companies still show the good elements of the first three innovation strategies in various combinations today. But the lab function has been opened up and transformed into the current campus models and open lab environments of multinational companies. Both Janssen Pharmaceutical companies of Johnson & Johnson and High Tech Campus Eindhoven are proven examples of the success of an open innovation ecosystem.

Hedging Strategy — The Philosophy of Hope

Clearly over the past ten years the positive elements of hedging have remained, and corporate R&D still has a budget for central, long-term developments. Some R&D activities need to be nurtured and hedged from daily business operations. The corporate R&D spend on innovation is a sizeable percentage of turnover, e.g. 10% of the total R&D budget. This percentage emphasizes the development of competencies for the long term. The other 90% of the R&D budget is allocated to strengthening the competencies to serve the existing business lines. In the earlier days the philosophy was "bring a number of brilliant scientists and engineers together, provide them with the time and the resources, and results will follow automatically" (Roussel *et al.*, 1991), also commonly referred to as the philosophy of hope. This has long been the legitimization for many firms to isolate the R&D function from the daily distractions of sales, operations and marketing. R&D has always been visualized by means of a central unit, laboratory or R&D site location.

The presence of a R&D laboratory or site was iconic, including the role of the classical R&D manager who is skilled in technological domains and primarily responsible for the heartbeat of corporate R&D. The R&D manager reported directly to the board of directors. The budget was determined by the confidence in science and technology and the firm's turnover and growth potential. Under this strategy, the cost of R&D is part of the budget of the corporate board, or otherwise financed and divided among the divisions without discussion. Within the hedge of central R&D, the organization unmistakably shows features of the professional bureaucracy (Mintzberg, 1979). The unity of control is at a central level for R&D activities and top management commitment to the corporate projects, especially from senior management. Also characteristic of this strategy is an efficient and well-planned R&D portfolio and no alignment to short-term business goals. The synergy between the science and technology disciplines was conducive to R&D performance. Looking at innovation in this way, the organization bears much resemblance to a university.

R&D hedged in a functional unit has the potential disadvantage of creating functional barriers between all other, relevant departments, for example between production and marketing. These barriers can result because of:

- A disconnect with market needs and changing priorities.
- A lack of common goals and unclear responsibilities between functions.
- Control systems that evaluate activities differently.

The companies in this study have left the hedging model years ago and have taken major steps towards more effective models for innovation.

R&D Programming Strategy — The Relay Race and the Rising Role of Business Divisions

In case of rising turnover, profit and growing divisions, the division management is more powerful. This puts pressure upon the demands and corporate R&D spend, questioning its value for money. The R&D programming strategy introduced control systems such as project evaluation and review techniques, and steering and control instruments to monitor the input and output of the R&D expenditures. With the exception of a new control system, the internal organization of the R&D department retained the same structure. This suggests that innovation proceeds along an orderly, predictable sequential way in an attempt to minimize the risks. It's similar to a linear model that assumes a step-by-step sequence of actions. A research activity was completed and the outcome was "handed over" to the next department, e.g. development. The relay race is a good sports-based metaphor for this way of working.

Connect and develop

Practical evidence has emerged showing the shortcomings and problems of managing innovation as a linear process (e.g. Anthony (2006); Clark & Wheelwright (1993); Fuchs & Schreier (2011); Huston & Sakkab (2006); Leenders & Wierenga (2008); Rigby (2009); Ulwick (2002)). The main difficulty arose in managing the interface moments, especially the linkage between R&D and marketing. At each interface, and at each decision point every idea, concept or product feature was specified in detail before being handed over. But this assumption did not seem to be valid in real life. Such a transition from one stage to another can be compared to a relay race. At critical moments, handing over the stick ("throughput") to the next stage failed. In the relay race a lot of time was wasted on such hand-over moments. The interfaces could thus become the bottleneck in each innovation stage with the ultimate consequence of delay. There appeared to be a need to connect and develop, for example for streamlining activities to better organize the part–whole relation of activities.

Through this perspective the development process is regarded as a sequential process. In addition, the decision moments for "Go" and "No Go" were clearly indicated (Cooper's (1994) "stage–gate model"). Division of tasks, standardization and formalization are viewed as ingredients to the effectiveness. Additionally, the innovation chain itself appeared to be clogged up by bureaucracy and formal control. Under this strategy, part of the corporate R&D funds are earmarked for projects formulated in conjunction with the divisions. There exist differences between the firms in this book in this sense, primarily explained by the stage and age of the company. In the chemical sector, R&D is decentralized, breaking away from the programming phase. Even more it is accompanied by a leading innovation business line for long-term growth. Similar changes can be observed in the pharmaceuticals industry; the development functions are nowadays forced to investigate new medical domains.

Streamlining Strategy — Mandate and Power to the Teams

Already in the early 2000s the evidence of the programming approach diminished greatly. A large number of leading American and European firms fell behind their Japanese competitors both technologically and commercially. The innovation function had become too isolated from the market. A closer look at the past ten years at the leading companies in this book reveals that the programming strategy has been left behind. But the good things have been strengthened e.g. stage–gate for venturing and sustainability rules (e.g. ECO+ solutions) and the cross-function flow of knowledge. The quality of the team is a driver in the success of innovative projects (Engwall, 2002; Hoegl & Gemuenden, 2001). No project is an island and the role of teams gained enough evidence as a powerful way to generate new knowledge.

Multidisciplinary team design and dysfunctions

Multidisciplinary team concepts appear in various forms, such as rugby teams (Takeuchi & Nonaka, 1986), skunkworks

(Quinn, 1999) or venture teams. Skunkwork teams are highly innovative, fast-moving, and slightly eccentric activities operating at the edges of the corporate world. The origins of skunkworks go back to a development team at Lockheed's design and development center. These cross-functional teams operate for a certain period on a new product concept and are fully detached from the regular organization and daily practice. They often have a separate location and work under tight deadlines. In contrast, venture teams operate in an environment with high-risk endeavors. It is uncertain whether or not this specific team approach is favorable above other team structures, as they are infrequently used for new product development.

Many studies identified practices that support team learning and their impact on speed to market (Huizenga, 2004; Lynn *et al.*, 1999; Volberda *et al.*, 2013). Clark and Wheelwright (1993) introduced the concept of heavyweight project teams, which is typical of large-scale innovation projects. Heavyweight project teams are multidisciplinary teams with a heavyweight project leader who acts as a powerful linking pin and coordinates the activities of the product development team, but also works with senior management to create an overarching product concept. In this concept the senior management can exercise subtle control through such project leaders, who manage the multidisciplinary team in the context of a clear vision. This type of team structure offers improved communication, stronger identification with and commitment to a project target, and a focus on cross-functional problem solving. Lencioni (2002) wrote the *Five Dysfunctions of Teams* and explored the fundamental causes of organizational politics and team failure. He provided arguments on the theme of team power and the struggle to be an effective team. For Lencioni, teams are frustrated by five factors and it requires compassion and dedication to be successful as a team:

- Absence of trust. A key driver of team dysfunctions residing in the unwillingness to be vulnerable within the group.
- Fear of conflict. In particular seeking artificial harmony over constructive passionate debate.
- Lack of commitment. This aspect is about simulating buy-in for group decisions that creates ambiguity throughout the organization.
- Avoidance of accountability. This is about ducking the responsibility to call peers to account about counterproductive behavior which sets low standards. Teams are mediocre because they delegate work, miss deadlines, and team members dislike the performance differences between the members of the team.
- Lack of attention to results. More particular focussing on personal success, status and ego before team success. These are the hurdles for effective teamwork.

Lencioni states it is not a question of know-how and knowledge but one of courage. Teams are effective if they share a common goal and a dependency upon each other to reach the goal (McDonough III, 2001). Let us dwell a little bit more into the goals of teams in the case examples.

The All Blacks rugby team

The story of, for example, DSM shows that innovation is also a story of team sports like rugby. The exemplary stories of Dyneema® and ®Claryl show how a new business team is expanding the product horizon. Dyneema® delivered innovations in multiple application areas, e.g. in performance textiles.

One of the landmarks was the Olympics Games of 2012 in London when the Dyneema® fibers were used extensively in the ultra-modern cycling suits. The team of ®Claryl delivered, amongst other areas, a breakthrough in the realm of the solar panel segment. The teams envisaged the end line ahead, but the road to get there was still open. In order to get there, the team had to make steps forward and backward. Metaphorically new business teams resemble a rugby approach, where team players are high-performance oriented, and jointly proceed forward to the end line. Learning from lessons the team has made, the players take a step back, evaluate the investments in resources, and check the market volume which has been created. Exemplary of this is one of the most famous rugby teams in the world, New Zealand men's national rugby union team, known as the All Blacks. The All Blacks are the current holders of the Rugby World Cup and were the 2013 International Rugby Board Team of the Year. They have won over 75% of their matches and are the leading match point scorers of all time. They are the only international side with a winning record against every country they have played. Since their international debut in 1903 only five nations have defeated New Zealand in test matches. Since the introduction of the world rankings in October 2003, New Zealand has held the number one ranking longer than all other teams combined. What is the secret of this team? Of course there is the role played by the Haka, a traditional Maori dance from New Zealand. But the five key functions of teams from Lencioni are also included in their team approach: trust, seek constructive and passionate debate on tactics, be results driven, maintain high standards and, of course, legendary status.

Let us now find out how and why teams are used for business innovation.

Power Teams — Ninja Innovation, Avatar Teams, Heavyweight Project Teams, Value Teams

Large companies are used to relying on market research to design and size markets and ensure correct strategy decision. But the search for tomorrow's business has to be conducted close to the market. A painful and risky venture? Markets that do not yet exist are difficult to measure and analyze, so the team should spend as much time as possible with prospective customers, partners and suppliers. Best-in-class stories and lessons come when a team goes beyond talking, to actually attempting to research, develop, produce, sell and support its offering, even if the offering has some limitations.

Nowadays we often see the team concept in action. Shapiro (2013) described the concept in the form of a killer strategy in his revelation of ten secrets of "ninja innovators" like Apple, Amazon, Google and Microsoft. These are companies that are successful, even legendary, in the scale of their innovations. Their ninja strategy is characterized by:

- Strength.
- Survival.
- Cunning.
- Intensity.
- Adaptability.

We can conclude from the practices of the companies described in previous chapters that the mandate for innovation is nowadays predominantly with the teams; more explicitly, powerful, knowledge-intensive teams with far-reaching responsibilities, instead of the formal control systems that seem to act as a brake rather than an accelerator. Let us take some example practices to take a closer look.

Power of a value team to create a breakthrough in the business model

Value teams have the mandate to search for new value propositions in a certain market domain. They are equipped with the resources to look for new customer insights and transfer the current product–market combination towards these new value propositions. For example the use of "value teams" by Janssen in Germany was aimed at finding new value propositions in the area of pharmaceuticals. Propositions for cost reductions in therapeutic domains are of incredible importance. Janssen started to work with performance contracts in the domain of psychiatry. Their value proposition was directed at a 360 degree patient care cycle, combined with cost reductions in the treatment process. Together with a German insurance company they created a new value proposition.

The practise of the avatar team to get inspired and gain insights

The metaphor of avatars is used to gain deep knowledge of customer needs. In Hinduism, an avatar is a deity descended to earth in a human incarnation, although following use in films such as *The Matrix* and *Avatar* the word has come to mean incarnation in human form more generally. The metaphor of avatars is used to characterize the search for new ideas from other industries.

How can we gain new business insights? Several teams of multidisciplinary functions from Janssen obtained an assignment to learn from other companies in other industries, e.g. ColaLife. The teams gained new ideas and insights on market trends and company tactics. This inspired the people from Janssen to look at their own business from a new angle.

Heavyweight teams with a mission critical mandate

An example of a heavyweight team is the Janssen team working against Alzheimer's disease. Both a scientific manager and a commercial manager co-chair the knowledge development of this therapeutic area. They are responsible with a team of approximately five to six key scientists who have a mandate to search for solutions in therapeutic areas. They try to discover the existing knowledge on protein, the technology of imaging to detect protein, the experts on neurosciences and neurological imaging. They are mandated to make joint collaboration agreements with imaging technology providers like General Electric and Siemens.

The core team in search of breakthrough discoveries

How can scientific breakthroughs be made? The Newtricious core team is mandated to start the journey in search of the egg nutrition discovery. This team concept is enhanced by in-house R&D people and also surrounded by a network of consultations and scientific institutions.

Classical cases of Japanese companies like NEC, Xerox, Honda and Nissan (Nonaka & Takeuchi, 1996) have already revealed the effective use of multidisciplinary teams. There, multidisciplinary teams were predominantly used in the pre-development stage. Once the design of the product was clear the team split up and the activities continued to be performed by functional groups working in parallel on parts of the work. The groups ensured sufficient functional knowledge input from the various functional disciplines in the pre-development stage. This method resembles an American football game. In American football, teamwork and individual actions go hand in hand within a pre-defined set of rules.

It is imperative that innovation is viewed as a process that runs upstream from the conception of a product to the go-to-market and distribution downstream. It is not a sequential, but an iterative process, in which development phases purposefully overlap and functions cooperate with one another intensively. This leads to a complex set of measures in many firms which aims to streamline the innovation function. Bureaucratic obstacles are removed, dead weight is rejected, and vigorous management must ensure that "good ideas" are piloted to the market as quickly as possible.

Innovation is no longer the sole task of one functional department, followed by the next department. Knowledge development has come to involve more functional disciplines at the same time. In this perspective, innovation is all about team efforts, like rugby, where team players jointly proceed forward to the end line. The main differences between a relay race and other team approaches, in terms of innovation, is the presence of overlapping development stages, and the early cooperation of various functional disciplines even at the pre-development stage.

Ultimately, teams are a crucial ingredient to success, both within the organization and in connecting to partners in the supply chain and the customer. High Tech Campus Eindhoven and the Janssen innovation campus provide a fruitful ecosystem within which to enhance the connection of disciplines.

The Collaborative Strategy — Customer Focus and Open Innovation

All companies like DSM, Janssen Pharmaceutical companies of Johnson & Johnson, High Tech Campus Eindhoven and Newtricious have proven successful in adopting the open model for innovation. They actually share knowledge with others and jointly reap the benefits from innovation. This requires the following steps.

Common denominator — ambitions to create customer impact

The company stories have one thing in common. Solving unmet customer needs is the ambition level of all companies. Janssen is pursuing, for example, catering to unmet medical needs. DSM is pursuing the wish to impact people's lives to create a brighter living. A dominant perspective for innovation is the focus on the customer:

- Create an impact on people's lives.
- Create an impact on societal needs.
- Create an impact on the health and well-being of people
- Meet unmet customer and medical needs.

Cooperation in the chain

The relationship between supplier and customer plays an important role in the streamlining strategy. The supplier views the customer more and more often as a source of new ideas (von Hippel, 1988). The suppliers are becoming problem solvers, who get under the skin of their customers in order to be able to provide a complete package of products and services. They try to get a clear picture of the "customer's customer." There are several ways to do this:

- Improving communication with the customer.
- Observing consumer behavior.
- Being present in the end-market.
- Sharing development programs.
- Customer feedback (this is great for telling what went wrong, but not what you should do next).

In most cases, this development implies a gradual change in the economic exchange relationship between customer and supplier, from a market relationship towards an organizational relationship and, ultimately, even an engaged relationship. The line of horizontal organization is continued, so to speak, beyond the boundary of the corporation. Mutual trust is vital. Sometimes it will be the supplier who faces major uncertainties, sometimes it will be the customer. For example, a supplier specialized in chemistry or engineering is expected to attach great importance to the reliability of its customers, while for bulk producers the reliability of suppliers is far more relevant.

This strategy implicates that the innovation function is streamlined in organizational terms, and not only because the knowledge flow is chosen as a point of departure. The aim is to reduce the management burden by drastically reducing the organization's complexity. At the same time, the flexibility needed to respond to and anticipate changes in the market increases. The above-mentioned components contribute to this. The focus on "core business units" cuts off useless side roads. Cutting back long-term R&D diminishes the incessant tension between what should be finished today and what the future promises. Giving priority to the project flow above the functional flows creates clarity. Finally, decentralization to the business unit ties research, product development and production closer to the customer. The consequences of interventions will become visible more rapidly and hence it will become easier to steer the process.

Streamline, Disrupt, Connect and Develop

All of the participating firms have experienced an intensive organizational change throughout the past years and reconceived their change process (Balogun & Jenkins, 2003). Time periods of four to five years mark the stepping stones in the change process. Safeguarding, consolidating and underpinning their position as a thought leader or market leader, was the driving force behind this renewal in all the firms. The change was not created by a sense of urgency, e.g. declining market share, turnover or profits. Primarily the strategic foresight of the companies led the change process. The quest for value in the shape of pharmaceuticals, food or science breakthroughs is characteristic for all companies.

Companies such as Janssen Pharmaceutical companies and DSM made a solid start from a relatively comfortable position with positive returns. For companies like Newtricious and High Tech Campus Eindhoven, their starting position was different, visionary, first-moving and challenging. Showing the evidence of an effective business model was their first concern. For Newtricious, the youngest firm, finding scientific breakthroughs was a challenge early in the company development.

Immelt *et al.* (2009) indicated the strategic foresight of General Electric and how this company disrupts itself and creates innovation. Huston and Sakkab (2006) described the essential importance of "connect and develop" for Procter & Gamble's new model for innovation. Although the companies in this book reside in different industries, their starting position is similar. This position primarily resides in the efforts and commitment built up in the firms to initiate the change process. In addition, all of the participating firms have set out on a comparable track, regardless of the business in which they operate.

Table 1 provides an overview of the key drivers observed in the company strategies. This "streamlining" process has been prompted in all of the firms by changes in the business environment. A beacon in this streamlining process is deep insights

Table 1. Overview of innovation strategies and drivers for the transformation of the company.

	Royal DSM	Janssen Pharmaceutical companies of Johnson & Johnson	High Tech Campus Eindhoven	Newtricious
Regenerate corporate strategy and reinvent industry	• Brand promise: "Bright Science. Brighter Living.™"	• Corporate credo: "Our first responsibility is to the doctors, nurses, patients, the mothers and fathers, and all who use our products."	• High Tech Campus Eindhoven: innovation in the hub and the "smartest region of the world."	• Newtricious' mission is to contribute to a better world, through the development of unique scientific knowledge in the field of functional foods.
Type of innovation	• Open innovation, venturing, and a structured approach to emerging business areas. • Campus model and international presence.	• Collaborative innovation — ""the world is our lab." Moving Frontiers with the Janssen campus strategy. • Campus model and international presence.	• Open innovation ecosystem and is part of the internationally awarded 2012 "smartest region of the world". • Ecosystem for innovation resident on 1 km^2.	• Principles of open innovation. Shift from a small R&D model towards an open model innovation. • Network of science institutions.

(*Continued*)

Table 1. (*Continued*)

	Royal DSM	Janssen Pharmaceutical companies of Johnson & Johnson	High Tech Campus Eindhoven	Newtricious
			• Ecosystem is characterized by partnerships boosted by the open research programs of technology institutes like Holst Centre, ExperienceLab, EIT ICT Labs, and Solliance.	
Innovation in the business model	• Ability to change as a core competency. • Innovation center. • Emerging business areas. • Venture center.	Core competencies and patient-centric approach on five therapeutic areas: • Neurosciences. • Oncology.	Amongst the ambitious goals for further growth are: • Expanding the range of locations and facilities with new accommodations,	• Inspired by Darwin. It is not the strongest of the species that survives, nor the most intelligent that survives. It is the one that is the most responsive to change.

(*Continued*)

Table 1. (*Continued*)

	Royal DSM	Janssen Pharmaceutical companies of Johnson & Johnson	High Tech Campus Eindhoven	Newtricious
	• Senior leadership role for chief innovation officer and chief technology officer.	• Vaccines and infectious diseases, • Immunology. • Cardiovascular and metabolic disorders.	• New companies entering the ecosystem. • Attracting investors and venture capitalists, in order to support the starters.	• End-consumer research. • Value chain analysis of the entire chain. • Retail analysis.
Guiding principles	• The seven principles of innovation. 1. The portfolio of core competencies and “know-how to scale.”	• The five innovation rules. 1. Innovation rule #1: dedication to meeting unmet medical needs.	• Foster over 100 SMEs in the High Tech region that participate in network clusters on domain of high tech.	• Entrepreneurial CEO with innovation core team. • Strong ties to scientific institutions and universities.

(*Continued*)

Table 1. (*Continued*)

	Royal DSM	Janssen Pharmaceutical companies of Johnson & Johnson	High Tech Campus Eindhoven	Newtricious
	2. The strategic council. 3. A corporate science council and its knowledge principles. 4. A DSM science network model. 5. The guidance by the core competency area plan. 6. The central business role for the innovation center. 7. The growth areas and management of the emerging business areas.	2. Innovation rule #2: focus on solutions for the five therapeutic areas. 3. Innovation rule #3: collaborative innovation — "the world is our lab." 4. Innovation rule #4: core competency and team focus on disease strongholds. 5. Innovation rule #5: getting proof of concept.	• Environment fostering influx from value-adding partners, crossing value chains and technologies extending the geographical campus surroundings. • Developing collaborative consortia with start-ups, and global corporations. • Business model of open (corporate) innovation facilities (e.g. Holst Centre) and positioned in the high-tech market as a unique framework for consumer insights, sustainability, behavior	• In-house R&D knowledge. • Collaborative innovation in pre-development stage with multinationals.

(*Continued*)

Table 1. (*Continued*)

	Royal DSM	Janssen Pharmaceutical companies of Johnson & Johnson	High Tech Campus Eindhoven	Newtricious
			and user-centered break-away innovations.	
Ecosystem for innovation and R&D model	• R&D efforts guided by strategy council and science council. • The R&D organization has a global presence with over 30 different R&D locations. DSM has opened three research labs in China — including the DSM China campus.	• Become number one in therapeutic strongholds. R&D is directed towards five disease strongholds. • Strong role for innovation campus. • Venture and incubation center (VIC) boosts business development. • Entrepreneurship.	• Expanding the ecosystem is managed along three knowledge domains: acquire new competencies, incorporate new technologies and new areas of applications. • Research programs coincide with open collaboration programs to foster R&D.	• R&D journey of five years, subject to three years by performing clinical trials. Co-creation with scientific institutions.

gained from strategic scenarios of major market and social trends.

Deep dives — scenario analysis on the society and technology trends

The position of the company in the value chain is an essential point of reflection. The companies need to know what is happening at the customer side. It is also important to be aware of the issues and changes on the supplier side. This provides insights into the advantages and disadvantages of the company in the value chain and the position against the competitors. This deep analysis of the strategy and the business model is not a yearly activity. Both DSM, Janssen Pharmaceuticals, and Newtricious perform such "deep dives" (scenario analysis) once every three to five years. This is a remarkable finding, because these companies constantly question their revenue model. Deep dives also address the crucial questions on what customers actually value, and how to make money.

This deep dive activity is conducted in collaboration with management teams in order to foster an involvement in the process as well as an acceptance of its outcomes. Insights into the trends provide answers to the fundamental question of the current business model and the value-creation strategy. Both societal developments as well as technological developments determine the future of the revenue model. Technological trends can be forecasted and are aligned with the major trends in society.

Such deep dives describe the major global demographic and societal trends. Among these trends the companies observe global shifts, climate and energy changes, and health and well-being concerns across the world. Global shifts include the constant demographic shift of wealth from West to East and from North to South, as well as a trend towards an increasingly older, increasingly urban, increasingly connected, and increasingly wealthy global population. New, major challenges in the field of climate and energy include the scarce resources and grasping the potential of bio-based fuels. All companies identify the growing interest in answering the societal question of securing health and well-being for people. The aging population, the medical challenges, the potential of upcoming intelligent materials and technologies are of strategic relevance to the companies.

The deep dives on the society trends (e.g. DSM, Newtricious) provide solutions areas for new products and services. Companies transformed their portfolio based upon the strategic trends discussion. The outcomes of deep dives have a profound impact on the organization. They give directions to the long-term developments of the organization, market expectations and new revenue models. It guides decision making on investments, resource allocation, and exploring and divesting in market segments.

Ecosystem for Open Innovation

Open innovation is a complex and risky process. The pressures are high. While product life cycles tend to become shorter and shorter, time-to-market has become crucial. Companies are urged to see their returns fast. For decades managers and professionals have been looking for tools and models to plan their innovative action and control the risks. One might regard this effort as an internal re-engineering and streamlining of the innovation process. Cooper's stage–gate model (2000), for example, has become a widely adapted approach in the world of practice.

However, one might ask whether these structured approaches have solved all the problems of modern times. The answer is clear: no. The business context has changed dramatically, setting new standards for product and technology development. But what is the next recipe for companies?

In recent years the common practice of innovation management has been re-evaluated in a critical sense. It has been regarded (Chesbrough 2003) as a predominantly internally oriented and closed process, based on the idea that "(...) if you want something done right, you've got to do it yourself." Chesbrough (2003) makes an intriguing case for *open innovation*:

> Rather than relying entirely on internal ideas to advance the business, an 'open' approach to innovation leverages internal *and* external sources of ideas. Rather than restricting innovations to a single path to market, open innovation inspires companies to find the most appropriate business model to commercialize a new offering.

This view implies a shift from "generation" to "connection," "engagement" and "collaboration."

Other scholars (Govindarajan & Trimble, 2004) argue in the same vein that innovation is rather a matter of learning and experimenting than of planning and control. One can identify various levels of open innovation between companies and their customers. Certainly, literature advocates the open innovation paradigm (Chesbrough, 2003; Huizenga, 2004; Prahalad & Ramaswamy, 2003). Birkinshaw *et al.* (2011) warn us not to follow the popular recipes for improving the innovation process uncritically. From a business perspective it is evident that open innovation is a solid route taken by each of the companies in this book (see Table 1).

- A lab ecosystem for the high-tech sector. The ecosystem for open innovation flourishes in the high-tech sector exemplified by the business activities at High Tech Campus Eindhoven. It created a powerful R&D cluster, and became one of the largest science parks in the world. At High Tech Campus Eindhoven, partnerships are boosted by the open research programs of technology institutes like the Holst Centre and the various labs and the research programs.

- Janssen Pharmaceutical companies make a clear statement: in order to come up with innovative and differentiated products that will address unmet medical needs and in order to fill the pipeline continuously, the company needs to tap into the best science in the world, collaborate widely and review drastically the way R&D is performed. Amongst the strategic approaches taken is to invest in the model for open innovation with an entrepreneurial and open campus model, while ensuring the business operations improve their operational excellence.

It provides evidence that firms open up, combine internal and external paths to the market. The companies thus advance their technological competencies.

Sustainability is a part of the innovation game

Otto Scharmer and Katrin Kaufer (2013), extend their U-theory and state that companies need to update the economic logic to an ecosystem of awareness of well-being. We conclude the same fundamental change for companies doing business, one that is more resilient, intentional, inclusive and aware of society engagement. Another theme in common between the firms is the sustainability aspect of innovation. Each firm is in its own way contributing to the sustainability of society. Either by realizing a positive social impact (Johnson & Johnson) or by creating sustainable solutions to societal challenges. This is combined with realistic and ambitious goals to grow in new business areas and reduce their environmental footprints.

All companies commit and communicate a clear policy on the subject of sustainability. Even more, these companies have designed an explicit vision on the sustainability goals and have incorporated these goals in their innovation process. They, at certain milestones in the development of new products, ask the fundamental questions on their impact on and contribution to society. It has become a part of their strategic business plan or management of the new product portfolio.

For example, innovative new products not only serve as valuable business but also support DSM's sustainability targets. This company practice is dedicated to providing ECO+ solutions, which means that these — when considered over their entire life cycle — offer clear ecological benefits compared to the mainstream solutions they compete with. DSM has been one of the leaders in the Dow Jones Sustainability Index for many successive years.

Both High Tech Campus Eindhoven and DSM keep the people-planet-profit model as a control principle by means of an integrated approach. This approach is driven by:

- Paying attention to the environment.
- Paying attention to ecology.
- Encouraging sustainable and responsible solutions for society.

Ultimately, the companies share a vision on society and the planet. They endeavor to make innovations that will result in a sustainable, longer-lasting, safer and healthier society and environment.

All firms are leaders in their category. The common denominator is their ability to redefine their own business model and redefine the market boundaries in their respective industries. This comes down to:

- *Strategic foresight about emerging business opportunities.* The commitment to changing the industry boundaries.
- *Deep dives — scenario analysis on the society and technology trends.* Deep dive insights, based on strategic scenarios of major global demographic and societal trends.
- *Customer engagement.* A distinct customer-centered organization.
- *Lateral organization.* Decentralization of tasks and responsibilities to division, business units, and, within these, powerful business teams.
- *Ecosystem for open innovation.* Creating an outside–in way of working, creating openness and crossing organizational boundaries. Reinforcement of horizontal lines and reduction of functional (vertical) connections.
- *Collaboration* to cross organizational borders and start cooperation outside the value chain, e.g. with suppliers and technological ventures.

To use the terminology of Janssen Pharmaceutical companies of Johnson & Johnson, one might speak of a "rotation" of the organization.

Chapter 7

The Lateral Organization — Orchestrating for New Business

The Design of Lateral Linkages

Every organization structure has interior and exterior boundaries. External boundaries show (den Hertog & Huizenga 2000; Huizenga, 2004) where the organization stops and the market place ("the environment") begins. Interior boundaries demarcate the internal ordering and division of work. Various types of formal mechanisms can be used to link, or coordinate, the efforts of various organizational groups. The objective is to choose those structural linking mechanisms that provide adequate information flows, procedures and structures to deal with the innovation requirements. Formal linking mechanisms that are not sufficient to handle linking requirements will result in poorly coordinated work. Those linking mechanisms that are more extensive than needed will result in unnecessary cost, over-complexity or delays. Structural linking mechanisms can be analyzed in terms of their ability to handle information flows and complex problem-solving requirements, and explore emerging new business. The simplest form of structural linking is hierarchy: the formal distribution of power, authority and decision-making levels. Structural linking mechanisms like liaison roles and councils are cross-unit linkages that help to integrate and to cross permanent, temporary or *ad hoc* organizational boundaries. Innovation strategies require equal attention to several strategic aspects, for example, products, markets, emerging markets and geographies. Similarly, in highly uncertain environments with highly interdependent tasks, great pressures for coordination may come from both functional and production sides of the organization. Whenever strategy requires the simultaneous maximization of several dimensions (e.g. product, market, new business development) and/or when information processing requirements demand simultaneous consideration of these aspects, strong integrating roles are required. Essentially the innovation process is one of the most complex of all organizational processes.

Organizational boundaries can be an obstacle in the knowledge flow. Sometimes a step forward or a step backwards is needed, and mostly stopovers are inevitable because the corporate hierarchy is in charge of the business knowledge traffic. Moving frontiers, for example by merging business areas, questioning industry rules, or forming self-managing units, may be a remedy for part of the knowledge flows. However, new boundaries are bound to emerge between the new units. The following boundaries can be distinguished: inter-functional, inter-unit, hierarchical, geographical and exterior boundaries. The knowledge enterprise must develop the ability to give way to boundary-crossing knowledge traffic without burdening the business hierarchy. Galbraith (1994) refers to this ability as "lateral organizational competency." The formation of lateral linkages is an instrument with which to develop new competencies. In this chapter the various types and examples of lateral linkages are addressed, with focus on their design and implementation.

Innovation places paradoxical demands on the organization. The basic (and eternal) source of paradox is between the business lines, projects (customer demands) and the organizational functions (disciplines, specialities). On the one hand, we still see the organization should be organic and informal. The borders between organization domains should be as open as possible. Horizontal cooperation or streamlining is the key. At the same time we expect that planning and coordination are fully under control and that specialist knowledge is safeguarded and hedged. The organization is not a static object; it is better described as a process. The word "organizing" might be better to express the continuous movement of internal and external boundaries.

There is a prominent place for organization in explaining the key success factor for innovation. Among the success factors is the organizational design (Huizenga, 2004) and learning from strategic experiments (Govindarajan & Trimble, 2004). Firstly, organizations can learn from drawing organizational boundaries among competencies, product–market combinations or business units. Redrawing boundaries and adapting to market changes helps to stick close to the customer needs and viable models for generating profits. Secondly, companies thrive on corporate entrepreneurship. Entrepreneurship can take various forms and can be aligned with the strategy or structure of venturing and open innovation. Instead of letting the environment define the corporate strategy, companies should craft a strategy that defines the environment (Kim & Mauborgne, 2009). In the economic environment of continuous change, the capability to explore emerging opportunities by launching and learning from strategic experiments is critical to survival. Strategic experiments range from high-risk, high-reward ventures, collaborations with third parties on new technologies and a strategy of creative destruction. Remarkably the cases explored in this book show us that it is not a yearly wager without clearly defined markets and accompanying revenue models. On the contrary, it is a disciplined high-commitment approach to seek emerging business areas, which involves open-mind thinking, campus collaborations and experimenting with lead users. This entrepreneurial role is of strategic importance to the larger corporations. It is a balanced portfolio of mid-term and long-term investments from which to reap benefits from new markets and customer segments.

The importance of the organizational design for entrepreneurship and a learning organization that provides room for strategic experiments are among the key attributes of the knowledge enterprise.

Crossing Organizational Boundaries

Boundaries are established in each firm or institution. However, linking innovation projects to strategy is a delicate task. One needs to understand the strategic boundaries between order (steady state management) and chaos (a thriving culture for breakthroughs) in organizations (Englund & Graham, 1999; Leenders & Wierenga, 2008). The company's aim is to draw a line around a group of activities and the people that perform them. Exterior boundaries demarcate where the organization begins and where it stops. Interior boundaries show how an organization is ordered internally. The result is a division, business unit, factory, department, project group or a team. They are the entities of the organization. An organization can be ordered by classifying activities of the same type, e.g. marketing, research, production, operations. This classical type of a *functional organization* is based on the principle of functional concentration. Organizational boundaries can also be drawn around activities that are related to the same market segment, product, service or customers, resulting in the *product-centered* or *market-centered* organization. The basic argument behind drawing boundaries lies primarily in the steering of the organization. It is assumed that grouping certain activities leads to more effective steering of these activities. Two typical rudimentary steering elements can be recognized, regardless of the ordering principle applied, when drawing the boundaries (Tushman & Moore, 1988):

- A hierarchy that tells the employee who his colleagues are, who the boss is, and who is the boss' boss.
- Book keeping that shows the costs and profits of the entity.

Moreover, organizational boundaries reveal the identity of the organization: the basis for the entity's culture. The members of the organization identify with their entity either strongly or not so strongly. As time goes by, collective behavior patterns arise which are based on the norms and standards characteristic of the entity. Knowledge diffuses through communities (Sorck & Hill, 2000). The culture is the result of a largely autonomous process which is hard to influence. However, the boundaries may be shifted from one day to the next due to a formal decision, which organizations do constantly because circumstances keep changing. Activities and employees are regrouped to enlarge the effectiveness of the organization. The arguments for shifting boundaries are diverse, reinforce each other and are sometimes contradictory.

- *Upscaling*: by integrating functional competencies, cluster business groups with similar distribution channels, factories etc.

- *Bundling*: flexibility and decisiveness can be enhanced by bringing the basic functions closer to the market in a business unit or multifunctional team.
- *Unbundling*: the complexity of the organization is reduced by introducing parallel product flows or by hiving off activities.
- *Hedging*: new activities can be tackled without external interruption.
- *Venturing*: creating new business in areas that are outside the scope of the existing business groups — through scouting and managing new business areas. Accelerating innovation throughout the company. This can be achieved through support in the fields of licensing and venturing and the corporate research programs.
- *Redistribution*: the organization is rearranged to find a new balance of power.

Shifts in boundaries do not always lead to the intended effect, for example when they are based on political arguments and functional arguments are used to legitimize the political decision.

There exists another limitation to demarcating new organizational boundaries: when activities and people within separate units are brought together the need to coordinate a number of these activities across units will arise automatically. Differentiation has its price: the price for integrating the entities into a larger whole. Lawrence and Lorsch (1967) show that this development is strongly linked with the growth of the organization. In this growth, the organization first differentiates in internal functions, followed by differentiation in the relevant groups in its environment, for example regional sales and service subsidiaries, a group for business customers, or a polyclinic. Reintegration into self-managing units (such as business units) is a subsequent new ordering with the aim to reduce the enormous administrative burden resulting from differentiation. Yet integration into self-managing units itself may also be viewed as a form of differentiation: differentiation according to product–market combinations. Most of the examples presented in previous chapters make clear that the organization is in a constant flux of adapting to the new business context.

In contrast, the relevance of border-crossing knowledge traffic is strongly on the rise. The reasons for this have been previously mentioned in this book:

- The integration of products and services.
- The concern for unit-crossing core competencies.
- The importance of cross-fertilization in the developments of new products.
- Globalization.
- Increasing complexity of processes, products and services.

From this point of view, one might wonder whether an organization cannot do without boundaries or with fewer boundaries. A growing number of authors answer this question in the affirmative. Many point out, and we have seen in the cases in previous chapters, that organizational architecture is the result of continuous improvisation. In these cases the managers point to the increasing importance of self-generating networks and virtual organizations, whose members communicate in many ways.

The cases of this book take a pragmatic stance in the debate on open, collaborative innovation versus boundary-crossing (but inside) innovation. Organizational boundaries will continue to exist as long as there are hierarchical relations and responsibilities for results and budget in organizations. The increasing tendency to hold firms and units accountable for their results and behavior (for example, for polluting the environment) is a counter-force against the blurring of boundaries. Apart from this, it has been demonstrated that the removal and blurring of boundaries will evoke or reinforce new, other boundaries. Finally, the question is raised as to whether the fashionable terms used to describe the future organization can be used to formulate normative organization strategies. For example, a knowledge network is not a result of reorganizations. Networks are "introduced;" they develop on the basis of a number of organizational conditions. In short, we do not advocate a futuristic model of the "boundary-free knowledge enterprise." Instead, we argue in favor of the reinforcement of the ability to develop, transport and apply knowledge across organizational boundaries. Galbraith (1994) refers to this ability as the firm's "lateral organizational capability." The use of the organizational instruments that are at our service is referred to as *lateral organization.* This chapter will focus on the instrument of lateral groups. Lateral groups are defined as follows: groups composed of representatives from different organizational entities, focussing on the coordination of common activities, whereby the hierarchy is burdened as little as possible. These lateral linkages are applied for coordination purposes across five different types of organizational boundaries:

1. Functional boundaries.
2. Boundaries between business units.
3. Geographical boundaries.
4. Hierarchical boundaries.
5. Exterior boundaries.

Rothaermel and Hess (2010) argued in favor of creating cross-linkages and combining innovation strategies in tandem. Their four approaches include recruiting and retaining superior human capital, internal R&D spending, strategic alliance and acquisitions. Let us now delve into the notion of the organization as a carrier of knowledge.

The Organization as a Carrier of Knowledge

Individuals play an important role in the knowledge enterprise. They are the most important carriers of knowledge in the organization. The tacit knowledge they have acquired over the years makes knowledge-intensive companies vulnerable, because knowledge workers can be replaced only to a limited extent. It is extremely difficult in general to fill the gap in a specific knowledge area. The role of the individual is often strongly felt when breakthroughs are made in the established industry domain. Radical changes in the knowledge enterprise are often based on the imperturbable work of a pioneer, a whiz kid, who will hold on to his or her own ideas no matter what. These pioneers are not always understood in the organization. Because there is no room for their new ideas, the real "go getters" may leave the company to start their own business. That is how the computer firm Apple came into existence.

Nevertheless, such breakthroughs do not thrive on pioneers alone. The pioneers' ideas do not take root until they are vigorously propagated into the organization. This role is called "product champion." Additionally, radical breakthroughs, which are usually time-consuming and swallow up money, require protection from the top management. This is the role of the knowledge entrepreneur (or "godfather") who believes in the idea and is prepared to cover the risk because he is confident that it will lead to new opportunities. Finally, the significance of the role of the "gate keeper" is recognized in most knowledge-intensive firms: the man or woman who follows external new developments and introduces promising developments in the organization.

Thus, innovation does not thrive on one single person. A variety of roles must be fulfilled, even when radical and creative developments in knowledge are concerned to which the individual pioneer is central. In other words: knowledge development in a firm or institution is practically always an orchestrated effort. This holds true by definition of knowledge development which is based on the input of various individuals, functions, and organizational units. Knowledge development is mostly teamwork, and the organization can be viewed as a collective carrier of knowledge. This collective character can take three forms.

Connect and develop

Firstly, the total amount of knowledge of the organization can be connected and must be *more* than the sum of the knowledge of separate knowledge carriers. Huston and Sakkab (2006) describe the power of connect and develop, e.g. knowledge creation in Procter & Gamble's new innovation model. Not only do two people that connect know more than one, these two people also know more than two individuals. Teams know more than a set of individuals. The combination of knowledge leads to new knowledge. Suppose a new marketer is recruited who has set up a new distribution method in sector A. When the marketer cooperates with the salesman in the firm who knows market B inside out, the possibility arises to adapt this new method of distribution to market B (e.g. ColaLife). This is the transfer strategy. Characteristic of the organization is that knowledge is closely intertwined with other knowledge. Knowledge of individual carriers or groups of knowledge carriers is seldom found standing by itself, but is generally found in combination with other knowledge. It is these very combinations that produce positive effects. Thus, knowledge of quality management does not provide better quality unless it is combined with production knowledge. These combinations produce clusters of knowledge, which even for a small firm can be highly complex. Much of this knowledge has a tacit character. In addition, the knowledge elements are intertwined and highly specific (idiosyncratic) of the organization, product, service, process and market of the firm. This is what makes it so difficult to copy the internally available knowledge of an organization.

A second characteristic of organizational knowledge is that it has a *common character* for a large part. Knowledge is transferred in an organization, which can thus be shared. Basically, the common stock of knowledge within an organization is freely accessible to all of its members, which is an advantage of an organization compared to market relations. This enables the firm to deal with knowledge efficiently; it is not necessary to reinvent the wheel again and again. Practically all of the instruments mentioned in this book are used for the transfer and storage of collective knowledge, ranging from training program, automated knowledge databases, handbooks, lateral groups, and job rotation. There is one danger here: as knowledge within the organization is easier to transfer (when made explicit and codifyable), this knowledge can also be more easily copied by rival firms. Quality certification is a fine example here. If the procedures for garage A are laid down adequately, it is not difficult at all to introduce these in an adapted form in garage B.

Finally, the organizational character of knowledge is reflected in the way in which this knowledge is embedded within the *structures and processes* of the firm. Knowledge areas are covered by organizational units or combinations of units: the knowledge centers.

The Blue Ocean Strategy — The Art of Business Development

With an increasing number of businesses, governments and network organizations facing environmental and structural conditions, companies can no longer afford to follow the common practice of letting structure drive in all situations.

The challenges organizations face today only underscore the importance of understanding how strategy can shape the future business model. That is not to say, however, that the structuralist approach is no longer relevant. Take any company with multiple businesses. The idea of strategy as a driving factor first appeared when Chandler (1962) proposed that the choice of organizational structure depends upon the corporate strategy being pursued. Chandler's argument was based on a study of US firms over the period 1919–1959. The cases of General Motors, DuPont, Sears, Roebuck and Company, and Standard Oil of New Jersey showed that structural adjustments in the organization were implemented after strategic initiatives had been taken. These initiatives occurred in areas unrelated to the traditional lines of business: *new business development*. This study and later ones (Galbraith, 1994) found empirical evidence that firms first start diversification, which then leads to business units and divisionalization and the appearance of the multidivisional organization. The essence of their proposition is that the organizational structure is secondary to strategy. Kim and Mauborgne's (2009) "blue ocean" perspective clearly confirms that different business units face different structural conditions with different resources and capabilities and have different strategic mindsets. The art of business development is to overcome the restrictions created by organizing the business in a structure that is inflexible to adaptation. They argue — based on plenty of cases in which firms' strategies shaped industry structure, e.g. Ford's Model T to Nintendo's Wii, Apple's iTunes, Google's Google Glass — that companies can systematically reconstruct their industry and reverse the structure–strategy sequence. Their two-way strategy is establishes that:

- A structuralist approach will be a better fit for some units where the operation environment is stable.
- Whereas a reconstructionist approach will be more appropriate for others striving for innovation.

The two ocean approaches and assumptions are distinct, and neither is sufficient to deal with the diverse and changing business conditions that organizations face. The challenge for leaders is to ensure that a robust organizational model is created which endeavors to pursue innovation consistently. While there is no shortage of literature on issues of strategy and structure, the body of empirical evidence is less impressive.

Designing Lateral Linkages for Business Development

Transforming the organization and keeping pace in the innovation process requires different types of lateral linkages. These can take the form of either absorbing knowledge from external parties (technology, scientific discoveries, market access) or transferring knowledge within the organization. Lateral linkages can also contribute to concentrating the knowledge into one organizational unit (a team or incubator). By concentrating this knowledge the firm is capable of exploiting this knowledge to reach the business goal: a new product, a new therapeutic breakthrough. On the other hand, lateral linkages can be of importance to steer the strategic direction of research and development

(R&D). Especially in the case of a multinational organization it is crucial to align the research activities of different divisions. This alignment is also necessary to guard the core competency portfolio in R&D. This kind of lateral linkage is closely related to the appearance of corporate R&D programs. These can be programs oriented at scouting the global technology trends and emerging business areas, but can also be programs to strengthen R&D competencies and spark the creation of new combinations from one technology domain with another, e.g. material sciences. Take the company with multiple businesses, consisting of several business units. Each unit faces different market conditions with different resources and capabilities. They have different strategic mindsets. It is the R&D challenge to align the R&D competencies for all the units, as well guarding throughout the entire organization a coherent R&D competency portfolio.

The examples of Royal DSM, Newtricious and High Tech Campus Eindhoven, reveal a range of lateral linkages. The organizational model at DSM consists of a coherent set of lateral linkages, which clearly show a competency orientation. This DSM knowledge infrastructure is primarily managed by organizational instruments, ensuring a lateral flow of knowledge within the organization. High Tech Campus Eindhoven is a hub structure and has proven successful as a powerful R&D cluster and open innovation ecosystem, where research activities lead to new business creation. Janssen Pharmaceutical companies of Johnson & Johnson teach us that besides the organizational change, transformation is an ongoing journey to transform the culture, invest in personal development, be aware of the change resistance in people and provide a positive culture for change.

Taking into account the time horizon of the cases over the past five years we investigated the organization design and efforts of the corporations. Steering and controlling the knowledge infrastructure requires an intelligent governance structure. Layer by layer, this governance structure ensures the right execution of innovation. One crucial observation is that the established companies can develop radical innovations and protect their traditional businesses. The secret? Create lateral linkages and organizationally distinct units that are tightly integrated at the senior executive level. Similar to the idea espoused in *Ambidextrous Organization* (O'Reilly & Tushman, 2004) we discovered that the companies have actually been quite successful at both exploiting the present and exploring the future.

In the case studies we looked at the range of organizational ties of the corporations and found that they share important characteristics. In particular, they separate their new, exploratory units from their traditional, exploitative ones, allowing for different processes, structures and cultures. At the same time, they maintain tight links across units at the senior executive level. The companies manage organizational separation through a tightly integrated set of linkages. These linkages are powered by a senior team with a facilitating and guiding role. Similar to the idea of the "ambidextrous organizations," we believe these linkages provide a practical model for executives seeking an engaged and sustainable business model for the future.

The structure of lateral organizations allows cross-fertilization among units while simultaneously preventing cross-contamination. The tight coordination at the managerial level enables the flow of knowledge between units to share important resources like R&D budgets, science and technical expertise. The separate organizational status ensures that the new units are not overshadowed by the daily requirements and "business as usual." These units, primarily aimed at business development, have their own way of working, giving room for distinctive processes, structures and cultures. They can fully

Fig. 1. Main categories of lateral linkages.

focus on knowledge development and launching new businesses. Meanwhile the existing business units can focus on improving operations, incremental innovations of products, and serving their customers.

Basically we identify the following major categories of lateral linkages (see Fig. 1):

1. **Business development clusters**. Knowledge clusters, competency domains or geographic concentration of R&D activities, primarily aimed at crossing organizational boundaries.
2. **Strategic lateral linkages and councils**. Strategic lateral linkages are designed to ensure the organizational capability to insource knowledge outside the organization. These forms help to align central and decentralized R&D. This includes the empowerment of technology councils to ensure long-term R&D, and network structures to direct science developments to the daily business requirements.
3. **Centers of excellence and innovation hubs**. Open innovation is all about collaboration. Centers of excellence and hubs are trending topics in innovation.

Business Development Clusters

Knowledge is not developed according to a single fixed pattern. A variety of development patterns can be distinguished, which are often implicit. At the start, one tries to set out projected lines, but once the knowledge development process is running, it tends to be forgotten. The working method has become self-evident. This changes when the knowledge development leads to a dead end, or when one does not succeed in speeding up the development of knowledge. At that moment, one starts looking for strategies to get the development going. This is where insight into the different strategies of knowledge development proves its true value.

Ripple strategy

Let us use the metaphor of throwing a stone in the pond, in which the rippling effect shows how business development proceeds. This rippling visualizes how business development proceeds, and is what is called the "ripple strategy" (den Hertog & Huizenga, 2001). The starting point for his model is the most rudimentary strategy of circles and waves. Imagine the first circle represents the knowledge field controlled by the organization at a certain period in time. This knowledge is based on one specific discipline, technology or approach, and is developed from one place or central location in the organization: a business development cluster. By ensuring a constant inflow and outflow of knowledge from the center, a ripple or splash or even waves are created for, for example, technological development, new therapeutic domains to discover or ways to connect to interesting ventures.

The knowledge clusters are primarily aimed at arranging a constant flow of knowledge-crossing internal organization boundaries. The objectives of knowledge clusters can differ:

- Keeping a constant flow of functional knowledge to ensure the business portfolio strengths.
- Concentrate knowledge in a special domain defined for new business.

Keeping both objectives in mind, corporations center knowledge to fuel the strengths and capabilities of the firm. For example the knowledge clustered around pharmaceutical strongholds, like Janssen Pharmaceutical companies. These strongholds are the heartbeat of the business model. One of the strategic directions taken by the company was to refocus on specific therapeutic areas. Janssen held a strong position in certain therapeutic domains, including a promising portfolio of pre-market development products, patents, and go-to-market initiatives. The strategic direction included finding the answer to the question: are we doing the right thing right? Janssen opted to divest in certain therapeutic domains and focus on a strong set of growth areas. Key to this long-term approach is a disciplined portfolio management, maintaining focus on specific therapeutic areas, and building a critical mass of innovation in these disease strongholds.

In a similar way DSM demonstrates a competency orientation. This competency orientation is primarily managed by seven key organizational instruments ranging from networks council structures and the innovation center's role. With regard to knowledge clusters the corporate R&D strategy is responsible for managing a focussed portfolio of core competencies. These manifest themselves in clearly defined knowledge clusters including competency areas in biotechnology, advanced synthetic methods (organic chemicals), process technology and materials sciences.

In the case of Janssen Pharmaceutical companies, we observe a similar pattern. A crucial part of the Janssen campus strategy incorporates a business development cluster. This hub is characterized by the venture and incubation center (VIC) that boosts business development. In this strategy, the VIC mission is to explore and stimulate promising internal and external opportunities with the potential to generate new sustainable healthcare solutions. It tries to achieve this with three aligned activities.

- Launch moderate to significant new healthcare businesses (adjacent to the company strategy).
- Foster, deploy, and attract entrepreneurial talent.
- Build a collaborative community, embracing open innovation.

Strategic Lateral Linkages and Councils

Innovation is more than just R&D and go-to-market strategies. The R&D efforts of companies need to turn know-how into cash, intellectual property rights, new market propositions etc. Companies need to decide how to spend their investment budget in areas of R&D. They need to decide if research needs to be leveraged or if the development efforts should be supported. Most of the time the R&D budget is allocated to strengthening competencies. A substantial part is invested to scouting emerging business and business development. One of the key dilemmas is how much of the investment budget is allocated to the short-term needs of the business and the long-term needs to find new business. It is about the balance between incremental innovations and long-term innovations; the balance in new products or new market segments, or processes and technology development.

The short-term R&D investment particularly involve the steps to improve product features, eliminate process failures at customer or factory sites, or improve technical support services. Safeguarding the competency landscape is often the responsibility of the corporate function. Aligning these activities requires good cross-functional cooperation.

Managing this playing field is a combined responsibility of corporate research and the business units or division. Among the organizational forms and governance structures to do so are the strategic council, the heavyweight team model, networks crossing geographical borders and human resource practices.

The model of the strategic council

This is a governance model which represents the key responsibilities for R&D, such as DSM's strategic council chaired by the chief technology officer. Their role is to align the strategic developments in the DSM business groups and share competencies between business groups. Furthermore this lateral linkage helps to transfer knowledge from one knowledge domain to another, e.g. biotechnology which is applied in nutrition or pharmaceuticals.

The "heavyweight" team model

Not only can an established company renew itself through the creation of breakthrough products and processes, but it can do so without destroying or even hampering its traditional business. Creating lateral linkages in the organization is not easy, and can even be subject to learning-by-doing. But we observe from the cases in this book that the way a team structures itself, combining organizational separation with senior team integration, is a means to manage innovation. Cross-linkages appear between corporate and business unit R&D by means of temporary (multifunctional) teams or even heavyweight project teams. The basic guidelines include the following.

- Functional designs integrate project teams into the existing organizational and management structure.
- Cross-functional teams operate within the established organization but outside the existing management hierarchy.
- Special assignment and "ninja" mission critical teams, which are set up outside the established organization and management hierarchy.
- Heavyweight project teams that are structurally independent units. Each has its own processes, structures, and cultures, but they are all integrated into the existing management hierarchy.

Network models crossing the science and geographical borders

European corporations expand their business horizons towards Asia and the US in order to create global connections to science networks. Similar patterns are shown by DSM, Newtricious and High Tech Campus Eindhoven. In this model there is a strong link with which to connect to science sectors and the scientific knowledge being developed by the universities and scientific institutions and communities. For example, Newtricious built up strong ties to the science environment of the Wageningen University in order to make a strategic analysis of the added value of the eggs product. Even more they intensified the ties over the years. In 2002 they set up a program with the Wageningen University, joining a project of the Unilever in the field of protein towards functional food. Since then the company initiated a private consortium and endeavored to run a large European science project, including the University of Groningen.

Also exemplary for this networking model is the DSM corporate science council. This is an effective approach to tap into the science world. It is installed as a governance structure and platform of scientists to discuss the research programs. Such networks also help to scout new research areas of interest on a global scale. This lateral organization link both strengthens the existing R&D competencies and dedicates time to developing new competencies.

To tap into opportunities in (emerging) fast-growing markets and pioneer value segments in Asian countries, companies must learn the development, trends and business rules in countries like China and India.

The human capital factor and human resources practices

Explicit attention for human resources comes down to understanding the creation of tacit knowledge in the organization (Nonaka, 1994; Nonaka & Takeuchi, 1996). This notion suggests a policy role for human resources management in strengthening the ability to learn and to innovate in a company. Human resources management aims to facilitate the knowledge flow. This is an important policy instrument for the company to develop competencies throughout the organization, and does so in three ways. First of all, this is through training on the job, which helps in rapidly developing people's expertise and creating cross-functional capabilities in very diverse jobs. Secondly, it is done through the leadership and personal development instrument. Leadership and career development programs provide a significant contribution to mix and match disciplines through the organization. It allows employees to understand the range of responsibility. Thirdly, the recruitment and horizontal career paths are important tools for strengthening the lateral linkages and creating synergy between business lines and knowledge domains (e.g. therapeutic areas, food, nutrition).

Centers of Excellence and Innovation Hubs

In the past, internal R&D was a valuable asset, even a great entry barrier in many markets like the pharmaceutical and chemical markets. Only large corporations like the top ten global players in an industry could compete by doing the most R&D in their respective industries, and subsequently generating intellectual property rights, patents on products and technological applications (ranging from medications and drugs to materials and food and nutrition). Essentially this is a simple model for R&D benefits are directly reaped from the investments. Then why is internal R&D no longer an important strategic asset?

Open innovation is all about collaboration and knowledge diffusion is best applied in a community-centric model. With the current state of technology, a single-firm solution is a thing of the past. Specialist companies, knowledge institutes and governments are increasingly joining forces. Open innovation is the preferred work approach. Companies are able to focus on their core competencies and at the same time inspire one another by sharing knowledge, experience and facilities. As a result, innovations are achieved more rapidly, are more cost-efficient and are of better quality. This gives them a clear competitive edge in a highly competitive market.

The secret of the companies like DSM, High Tech Campus Eindhoven and Janssen Pharmaceutical companies of Johnson & Johnson lies in their fundamental shift in thinking about innovation. They have learned to make the change from inside–out models to collaborative models for innovation. Chesbrough *et al.* (2006) refer to the decline of the old model of "closed innovation" where firms adhered to the steady state management philosophy, e.g. successful innovation requires control. These days, however, the leading industrial enterprises have broken with this philosophy. Surprisingly, these companies conduct basic research on their own, but also get new ideas to market through a different process. This process is characterized by centers of excellence, open campus models, venturing and collaborative innovation.

- Johnson & Johnson institutionalized the core disciplines in R&D in a lab organization. The establishment of labs and innovation centers in Shanghai and San Diego helps in creating international science and business linkages to absorb new technological developments around the world.
- The Johnson & Johnson innovation centers have a science discovery role. They are the primary scouts to build relationships with start-ups, academic institutes and all other stakeholders involved in healthcare. The innovations centers' role is to discover and explore the best early-stage science in the external world and to close early-stage deals. There are four innovation centers, established in San Francisco, Boston, London and Shanghai. They are geographically distributed so that each center has full responsibility for its region.

As networks become bigger, the interconnections between players tend to cluster around just a few, also known as network hubs. The simplest way to identify hubs is to map out the relationships between all the players in the market — suppliers, partners, competitors, regulators, consumer groups, and any other influential parties — drawing lines to connect them. The more connections, the more intense the hub. Locations like Shanghai and Silicon Valley are exemplary for major innovation hubs. High Tech

Campus Eindhoven is a similar international hub for the high-tech industry. On the site there are over 120 businesses working on the products and technologies of tomorrow. Right from the start one of the objectives has been to create a fertile breeding ground for promising businesses. International corporations and start-ups join in one hub model and locate their operations in dedicated business and technology accelerator buildings. In order to nurture a hub environment for new starters and spinoffs and spinouts of existing companies, High Tech Campus Eindhoven particularly focuses on start-up technical companies.

Global presence also requires one to be aware of the regional hubs and get engaged in the hub developments. DSM China's innovation center is set up to be present and understand the regional opportunities and work closely with the accompanying knowledge network.

A similar hub model is the Janssen campus in Belgium, which operates like a center of excellence and integrates the R&D, supply chain, commercial and supporting functions within the worldwide group of Janssen Pharmaceutical companies. It comprises legal entities and sites in Belgium, employing highly qualified professionals. This hub model pursues to build an entrepreneurial community and make the transition to an open innovation model.

For many companies the R&D organization requires a global presence. Metaphorically speaking it is a worldwide virtual lab. For example the knowledge system of DSM thrives on bringing people together, scientists and business people, exchanging people and ideas, and executing joint projects, thus creating a connected science network. This network model thrives on sharing knowledge and competencies for the benefit of the global company. This virtual network philosophy incorporates all people within DSM and the people connected to DSM. The network is similar to a knowledge map; layering the science competencies and people with the external cooperation links to other firms and close ties with research institutes, like MIT in the US and China's research institutes. The science network is grounded in a philosophy of sharing, bringing together, and feeling connected and committed to DSM's vision for the future.

We can conclude that a key success factor for the open innovation model is the presence of global and supporting functions and an entrepreneurial community who are engaged in a joint strategy to take full advantage of the proximity, the trusting and enduring relationships, the knowledge density and the economies of scale.

Transition Leadership is Generated by Making Choices in a Learning Organization

Analysis of the firms in this book presents a comparable conclusion. It is important that each of the participating firms has put much energy into formulating the knowledge ambition. Strengthening the core competencies and exploring the emerging business areas in parallel has triggered off the enterprise. The firms explicitly point out the relevance of engagement and innovation, which is expressed particularly in coupling the firms' strategic objectives. This leads, as we have seen in the case studies, to a far-reaching reshuffling of the business portfolio. We discovered that the companies have actually been quite effective at simultaneously exploiting the present and exploring the future.

The formulation of the strategic ambitions of the companies raises the question of how the R&D and knowledge potential can be applied most effectively. It is for that purpose that the participating firms have invested in new instruments that go beyond the organizational boundaries that have been erected by business units or divisional structures. Lateral organizational linkages (e.g. knowledge cluster, strategic councils, network hubs and technology platforms) and boundary-crossing personnel management all play an important role here. Firms have made substantial progress over the past five years. The industrial firms emphasize the organization and decision making in terms of the utilization and allocation of R&D. All firms have put a great deal of effort into the development of lateral linkages and have initiated investments in the knowledge enterprise. They all aim to bundle the three instruments into a coherent configuration for the knowledge enterprise, in which the senior, central group or manager plays an orchestrating role. Remarkably, "new business development" has been cast into a separate organizational entity in most of the firms, usually operating next to the other business units or divisions. The business development group is given a separate status in most firms with short lines to the broad management, for example in the form of double roles: technology managers and councils who are also responsible for business development. The relations with the business units, however, are of crucial relevance in the firms studied.

Some managers and organization consultants come up with a toolkit filled with instruments when confronted with terms such as synergy and (new) business development and innovation management: portfolio techniques, return on investment calculations, innovation funnels, technology councils, skills maps etc. One message is clear from the managers in the firms: the transformation of the organization is a journey. In this respect the culture of the companies is moving closer towards an engaged organization. As several managers described it, "we are heading there, we are learning along the journey and we have only just started." Thus, they all view organizational learning and knowledge management as one of the cornerstones of their innovation and technology policies. The utilization of the synergy potential within and among business units and groups has become a policy priority in the firm. One might describe this challenge as the development of the knowledge enterprise. This development process should fulfill three vital preconditions: core competencies, orchestration of new business and innovation ambition.

Core competencies — corporate direction for "doing the right things right"

What know-how and skills (or core competencies) are of crucial importance to our firm and what do we want them to achieve? These two questions refer to the firm's mission and vision and accompanying strategy. For example, today DSM is positioned as a global life sciences and materials sciences company, communicating the brand promise of "Bright Science. Brighter Living.™" This company vision is leveraged by its core competencies and concentrates on the strategic pillars of (i) nutrition and pharmaceuticals (life sciences); and (ii) materials sciences. When the core competencies of a firm are not clearly defined one is unable to tell in which direction competencies are to be developed, and it will be very difficult to explore and utilize synergy in competencies. A focus as well as a "sense of urgency" is needed to give the quest for synergy any significance. This quest is a transformation in itself. First of all, it is a quest to find the answers to questions about the existing value of the current business model. But it is also the quest to make money and exploit the core competencies. We have seen that companies prove to be a leader in their industry if their business transformation is built on core competencies. It is not surprising in this context that most of the participating firms have picked up the philosophy of Hamel and Prahalad (1994) about core competencies and truly implemented this strategy. The resulting choices may have far-reaching consequences, such as:

- New investments and divestments in technological know-how.
- Selling company parts.
- Purchasing firms through venturing models.
- Establishing strategic joint ventures.
- Increased cooperation with universities and other suppliers of knowledge.

In addition to products and market, knowledge has thus become a decisive factor in composing the business portfolio. This vision has significant consequences for the decision-making and communication processes within the firm.

Orchestration for new business

We can learn from these corporations how they organized and learned to manage innovation strategically. It is not about steady state management. These companies have a strong innovation track record and have articulated a clear ambition. They guide their core competencies portfolio, they manage along the innovation rules (Janssen Pharmaceutical companies) or organizing principles (DSM) and keep the right balance of core business and new business (opportunities). This can be done in an innovation center, an open campus model or through venture management. These companies manage consistently across the enterprise based upon an integral framework (the credo). The company's future is driven by clear strategic efforts that are substantially allocated with time, cash, senior leader attention and prestigious goals. That is essentially what is meant by orchestration.

Innovation only provides new energy when energy is added to get the system going. A threshold must be overcome. To put it differently: as the independence of project groups, unit and divisions increase, it will be more difficult to keep a coherent competency portfolio. A small but advanced orchestration function can fulfill a vital role to evoke and maintain synergy. Such a team must be capable of assessing the plans of business units, recognizing opportunities for synergy, following external developments, and proposing ideas to the firm's management. In approaches such as these, one must prevent an old centralized structure from being built up again through a back door. Orchestrating calls for the skills of a tightrope walker. If the balance tips to one side, the orchestrator will lose his position, and the balance will continue to be unstable. Firms that have developed these skills (such as Newtricious) seem to be able to chart a forceful technological course.

In its central management, knowledge-based organizations use flat structures. For example, in pharmaceuticals, the traditional sequence of research, development, manufacturing and marketing is being replaced by synchrony, meaning that specialists from all these functions work together as a team. The avatar teams and heavyweight project teams work in parallel to breed such new business opportunities.

The quality of management — dialogue is key

Investment choices are not made in the participating firms in isolation from corporate headquarters, but come about in the dialogue with the most relevant central and decentralized actors. Councils for R&D strategy, science councils, venture and incubation centers, each one of these is an attempt to create dialogue between disciplines. This dialogue enforces the decision on R&D investments. Therefore, strategic choices are the result of a continuous process rather than of a once-only strategic analysis like they used to be. This places high demands upon the quality of the senior management, both at the corporate and at the unit level. Managers are expected to:

- Explore and stimulate promising internal and external opportunities with a potential to generate new sustainable solutions.
- Look beyond the boundaries of their own organizational domain or knowledge area.
- Be able to "really" cooperate in teams, in which conflicts of interests, differences in visions and conflicts are no exceptions.
- Be able to make the connections (as "linking pins") in the communication and decision making between various organizational levels.
- Mobilize entrepreneurship at several layers in the organization.
- Continue to think and orchestrate dialogue inside the organization and with the external players.

All of the firms fully underline the significance of an advanced management favorably disposed towards change. All the same, they have all encountered challenges in the change process. Sometimes comprehensive changes were not possible until the composition of management had changed. In other cases, the changing of the guard took place while the process was ongoing, or fresh blood from outside was taken on. This has led in most firms to more focussed attention on the leadership training of managers that are able to think in integral terms and keep moving forward. Because different organizational forms are required to develop different forms of innovation, organizational adaptation is an important managerial issue. Managers need to think beyond incremental innovations and to think about R&D and knowledge management in order to develop fundamentally new products, processes or product–market combinations. Organizational adaptation involves actions taken within the firm as well as a range of extra-organizational efforts including venturing, licensing, joint ventures and alliances. As innovation involves disruption to the status quo, managing change is always a managerial concern. In the innovation business, managers must know both what to do as well as how to implement required organizational changes. Over time this involves the development of leadership styles and a senior team that can create the conditions to facilitate both short-term efficiency and long-term adaptability. Therefore organizational learning and the quality of R&D management are at the heart of managing innovation. This can only be shaped by a senior team that is itself flexible and adaptive over time. The managers of the participating firms called upon a mindset change and the ability for organization learning. A true managerial challenge lies in ensuring the knowledge systems of the company work at an organization level and an individual level. One needs to take into account, for example, the R&D, marketing and operations employees' perspectives. A dialogue at all organizational levels helps to safeguard the outcomes of the innovation efforts, just as a deep commitment of the employees to redirecting the firm's focus is essential for the success of the growth path.

Innovation ambition: constantly rethink the business model

One of the secrets of transition leadership of companies is to find purpose and be ambitious. Purpose is the one thing that all leaders have in common. The best leaders recognize a common purpose, shared values and aligned vision, and constantly question the business model. A remarkable commonality is that each of the participating companies constantly questioned its business model. The company stories provide a deeper understanding of this transformation process. It is easier said than done. It is the corporate process in finding answers to the question: are we doing the right things (right) for a sustainable future? Sustainability's next frontier is tackling the significant issues that lie at the heart of competitive advantage and long-term viability of the business model of the firm. We have found evidence that the process includes the ability of management to bring their organization in a modus of transformation. Nagji and Tuff (2012) talk about the innovation ambition and identify three levels of business innovation (see Fig. 2):

- Core business innovation.
- Adjacent business innovation.
- Transformational business innovation.

Business innovations are transformational if they develop new products and assets, create new markets and fulfill unmet customer needs. It is about developing breakthroughs and inventing solutions for as yet unmet (customer) needs and emerging markets. How did the participating knowledge enterprises transform and succeed with sustainable, viable business models? They all invested in the long-term roadmap for transformational innovation. They took periods of many years, or even successive periods to explore new business areas. Take for example the strategy of DSM, which was marked by five-year strategic programs to direct vision and focus. In successive periods of five years the company organized for the next level of sustainable growth. In the "Vision 2005" program it concentrated on the turnaround

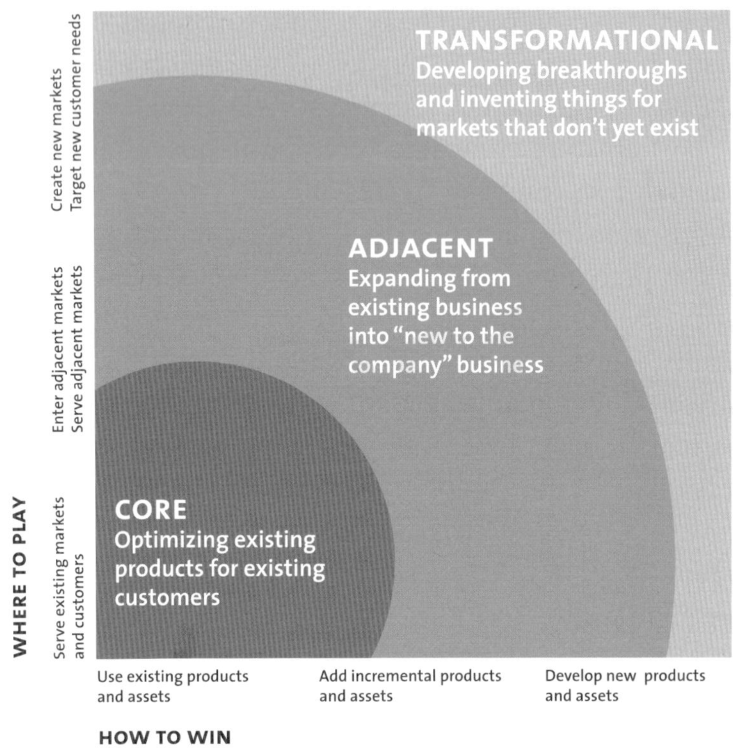

Fig. 2. The innovation ambition matrix. Reproduced with permission from "Managing your innovation portfolio" by Bansi Nagji & Geoff Tuff, *Harvard Business Review*, May 2012. Copyright (2012) by Harvard Business Publishing; all rights reserved.

from bulk to specialties. In the "Vision 2010" program, the strategic program focussed on reaping further potential from the company's portfolio transformation which took place from 2000 to 2005. DSM's "in motion" program was initiated when the company gained control of its portfolio of competencies and projects. Similarly, Newtricious built up its competencies and new business portfolio in successive periods between 1998 and 2006, guided by the scientific collaborations in nutrition and life sciences, and the company landmark moment in this period was when their first patent was requested.

Time to learn, time to understand the new market possibilities and time to develop knowledge and assets. The business cases in this book show us how the companies took actions in the organization and have a clear focus that unmet needs and nonexistent markets should be explored. The corporate mission is a firm statement, supported by investment power, in R&D or venture capital, to explore markets that do not yet exist and to target customer needs that are not yet met (see Fig. 2).

The creation of such an ambitious growth path is driven by companies that think in a lateral way about their current business model. These companies question their current business, scout emerging business areas and, above all, rethink and reinvent the industry boundaries. Companies learn to collaborate with stakeholders in the value chain and even more in unidentified markets to address sustainability issues on health, aging populations and bio-based economic dilemmas. Firms start to make sustainability-based models for innovation. For example, agricultural firms enter the knowledge domain of pharmaceuticals, and high-tech firms and chemical companies become solution providers in healthcare domains inspired by a brand promise for a better living. In this respect these companies are regenerating their corporate strategy, driven by innovation. Firms are aware of the need to develop new competencies and knowledge in respect of the increasing agility of innovation/market dynamics. Their growth strategies are driven by four main innovation drivers (Hamel & Prahalad, 1990, 1994):

- The strategic foresight, answering the ultimate question "are we doing the right things (right)."
- The ability to act — investments and divestments in their competencies and market portfolio.

- An enduring commitment to innovation and a long-term perspective for the transformation of their core competencies.
- Design a lateral organization structure and accompanying organizational process to transform and scout emerging and sustainable growth areas.
- Customer centricity, keeping in mind the unmet customer needs and society trends.

Successful companies show the ability to question their revenue model as an illustration of their lateral thinking of the organization's position.

Another way of entrepreneurial working at the basis

New business development and entrepreneurship cannot be prescribed by decree. Entrepreneurship and good ideas are generated because people on the shop floor "visit" each other and "shop" with each other; they look outside more often, and have escaped from the not-invented-here syndrome. Another way of working is a true reversal in culture in many organizations, e.g. Google, which calls not only for good leadership, but also for support throughout the organization. The opportunities to involve directly the workers at all levels or the organization in this undertaking should be exploited again and again. But how to mobilize this entrepreneurship? Idea generation is not the sole domain of R&D or of the innovation teams. The participating firms are committed to mobilizing idea generation throughout the organization, which has proved to be conducive to success (such as via ideas from avatar teams, ideas popping in the venturing and campus sites etc.) In a sense, the management is decentralizing innovation and passing responsibility to the individual: everyone can have a great idea, and everyone is supported in the generation of these ideas. In fact, more ideas make a better company. There is a potential for breakthrough ideas to occur through serendipity. The process is essentially a spark for corporate entrepreneurship. The management focuses on improving the talents and competencies of the human capital factor in the organization. Often, these opportunities naturally follow from daily practice (or from subtle directions), for example when:

- Personnel is temporarily exchanged in the case of an acquisition.
- Internal course programs are prepared.
- Project teams and work and study groups are composed.
- Information systems are set up.
- Salespersons and engineers approach the customer together.
- Other companies and knowledge centers, trade fairs and conferences are visited.
- New employees are trained.

These are occasions where employees temporarily leave their "fixed workplace" and are given the opportunity to look beyond their own boundaries and make their capabilities available to others.

The instruments of lateral linkages provide opportunities to make a new, entrepreneurial working method effective and efficient. These lessons can also be learned from the companies, like Janssen's entrepreneurial bootcamp and action learning programs and DSM's resource council that takes care of the talents in the DSM science population. The objectives of the resource council are to address the human resources management topics like:

- Locating the crucial skills, people, and talents flowing in the organization.

- Deciding how to rotate the skills and expertise in the organization.
- Planning how to nurture and develop the talent pool by means of career development and succession planning.

Assurance of knowledge of employees and an entrepreneurial culture are vitally important. Organizations and knowledge workers need a continuous stimulus or incentive to look beyond one's own boundaries.

Senior leadership and the orchestra performance

So long as companies manage innovation as a secretive, linear process, investments will be erratic and results disappointing. The managerial lessons from the industry leaders point out that it is time for an orchestrating and collaborative approach. Innovation on the other hand does not spring from a sole idea, a great scientist, a spinoff from a technology project, or inspirational thought. Innovating requires knowledge, inventiveness and above all orchestration to focus towards sustainable results.

Let us now consider the metaphor of orchestration and the conducting of a symphony, the director's role. The famous Dutch Royal Concert Orchestra performs musical programs based on two essential elements: tradition and constant renewal.

> The Royal Concertgebouw Orchestra is a symphony orchestra that gives orchestral performances of the highest caliber in the world's leading concert halls under the direction of the very best conductors. The activities it carries out in Amsterdam form the basis of its role as the Netherlands' ambassador for international excellence. The Royal Concertgebouw Orchestra [Dutch Royal Concert Orchestra] offers audiences emotional and intellectual enrichment, generating involvement and active loyalty. (Concertgebouw Orchestra, 2014)

It is one of the toughest challenges a management team can face: how do we create excellence? How to get our people to think creatively, to challenge the status quo, to renew, while still keeping everyday operations running smoothly? And in the meantime compose the good traditions and routines in the organization. One crucial role is that of the organizational leadership. Our understanding of the crucial role of organizational leadership has developed over time and we now identify several leadership modes, such as the level five leadership by Collins (2001) and the seven transformations of leadership by Rook and Torbert (2005). They provide the view of developmental psychologists, who agree that what differentiates leaders is not so much their philosophy of leadership, their personality, or their style of management, rather, it is their internal "action logic." It is the way they grasp and reflect upon their organizational surroundings and how they react in team setting and in occasions of authority, responsibility and power situations. From this perspective, "psychological pictures of leadership styles" are shown, which mirror one of seven developmental action logics. These seven are: the opportunist, diplomat, expert, achiever, individualist, strategist or alchemist. They resemble the key functions of a leader's dominant way of thinking.

By learning how the leaders in the corporation identify new growth areas, as certain new ideas, and assess new business areas, we uncover the corporate culture and capability to change. This essentially draws back to the corporation's ability to orchestrate the organization.

Drucker (1988) predicted the appearance of the so-called "information-based organization." He argued that instead of a control organization the new organizational mode is far more likely to resemble organizations that neither the practicing manager nor the management scholar pays much attention to today: the hospital, the university, the symphony orchestra. For each of these forms, typical business will be knowledge intensive, and the organization is composed primarily of highly professional specialists. These specialists direct and discipline their own performance and team performances are managed through organized feedback from colleagues, customers and central headquarters.

We have seen in previous chapters that the companies' practices have changed in time and in business context. Great leaders create the innovation culture by design; they will not allow culture to evolve by default. It is these characteristics that afford leaders a competitive advantage over those who don't understand the dynamics of these organizational linkages. Understanding the business context and the role of organizational linkages (design) is essential to understanding how companies orchestrate their new business development. Organizational change is often compared to the performance of jazz. Kamoche *et al.* (2003) describe the metaphor of organizational improvisation that even goes beyond the currently dominant jazz metaphor and look at music streams and symphonies in understanding the nature and complexity of organizational improvisation.

It was Drucker (1998) who first noted that companies are like orchestras in four essential senses:

- The knowledge and the knowledge workers (people).
- The instruments.
- The musical performances.
- The conductor.

Knowledge, capabilities and the people are the greatest asset of any organization. Without high-performing people a high-performing organization is impossible. These people must have the tools, resources and necessary senior support to do their jobs. Assuring these are in place is the primary task of senior leadership. As a consequence the senior leadership also chooses the direction of the (musical) performance. Ultimately, all these elements of "the orchestra" must be playing the same music. Using the orchestra as an organizational metaphor, we observe similarities between orchestrating a symphony and orchestrating for new business.

Firstly, the symphony can be resembled by the company's credo, its vision, mission and purpose of the organization. It is written down and guides the knowledge flows and knowledge workers. These are made explicit through its communication about the corporate strategies and tactics for innovation. Secondly, what holds this together and makes it work is the conductor. When we consider the organizational units, councils, campus residents and ventures of the corporations in this book, the concept of "orchestrating" reflects the functioning of the new business development function. This is a valuable insight to remember in order to understand how an organization is performing.

The case studies prove that the orchestration of the innovation function is not the sole answer to the organizational problems surrounding innovation. It is the combination which counts, e.g. the orchestrating inside and outside the firm's boundaries. Companies view orchestration and collaboration and open innovations as the crucial challenges. These challenges manifest themselves at the very moment companies are implementing the new strategy with plentiful energy: the challenge of balancing incremental versus radical innovation. Customer responsiveness, price and quality are not sufficient to survive as a large corporation in the longer term. In order to ensure one's position in the market of tomorrow and the day after tomorrow, the knowledge and resources from the entire corporation must be bundled to develop core competencies, which the firm can use to distinguish itself. At the same time the corporation explores emerging business areas. The question is whether the sharply focussed business units are able or inclined to support the kind of long-term research that generates or develops more radical ideas for new products, processes and services. The role of R&D is of crucial importance to book results both quickly and for the long term. Being close to the customer encourages incremental development, and rarely inspires breakthroughs, simply because customers tend to have an evolutionary view of their needs and rarely support a visionary spark. Yet a better understanding of the market demand and a focus on the unmet customer needs and aligning with the sustainability trends is considered to be important. These are changes that the firm must absorb and transfer internally. We underline that a strategic, independent, self-confident R&D function of critical mass is required to address new technological possibilities. Chief executive officers are involved in orchestrating the integration of technology in the corporate strategy, and the influence of the chief technology officers and chief innovation officers at the level of the board of directors is moreover much more powerful.

This has implications for the logic on which the knowledge strategies of the corporations are based. A number of firms understand these choices as being mutually exclusive options:

- Existing business areas, division and lines or emerging business areas.
- Meeting current customer needs or addressing unmet customer needs.
- More incremental research or more long-term research.

- More influence for the business units or more influence for corporate R&D.
- Market pull or technology push.
- Serving markets or creating markets.
- Product- and market-centered organization or functional organization.
- Being the boss in one's own business or synergy among businesses.
- Formal control or informal cooperation.

One might speak of a paradoxical approach here. Both are necessary and one cannot be excluded. Two contrasting arguments are presented and the decision maker is expected to choose either the first or the second argument. Paradoxes are not accepted, but must be resolved. Western management thinking is apparently based on a viewpoint that prescribes clarity, consonance and coherence. If one argument does not work, we will have to look for another scenario. And if that does not work either, perhaps we should revert to the initial scenario.

We use the word "orchestration" also in this connection. It refers to a dialectic style of organization development in which opposites produce a new synthesis through learning. The key question is whether harmonious consistent organizations can effectively respond to the inconsistent, conflicting and paradoxical demands imposed by the environment. It is increasingly argued that such environments call for a continuous state of creative tension, which keeps the firm alert, puts deep-rooted routines up for discussion, and continues to test accepted points of departure. In other words, replacing the "this or that" approach by the "both and" thinking. And this is one of the major drivers for the open innovation paradigm: stretch goals and look further into the future and leverage resources by cooperation.

It is not surprising that the leading firms, with an established reputation, have understood this orchestration message and perform by doing so. Yet industry leaders don't have a choice: if they want to continue to lead the market, they are forced to broaden their horizon. These companies are blending innovation with the most masterful ways of crossing organizational borders.

Bottom Line — Invest in the Art of Orchestration and the Lateral Organization to Ensure New Business

As stated earlier, this calls upon a new kind of innovation in companies, in terms of search for transformational, breakthrough, or game-changing innovation. The playing field is unclear. The rules are subtle and the end score, in terms of risk and financial returns, requires the corporation's willingness and senior commitment to explore unfamiliar assets and build competencies. It also requires an ambition, a company credo as a guideline to build competencies that are rooted in deeper understanding of unmet customer needs, and the willingness to begin the quest for new technologies that have no direct business evidence (yet) and to develop emerging market areas.

This kind of strategic renewal is not derived from a sole idea, a R&D event or a detailed program. Rather, it is a set of practices that can guide senior leaders into a new era of innovation. Business innovation and accompanying strategic renewal involves making changes ahead of the current business and competencies. Of course, the efforts can be extremely difficult to initiate, fund and lead. The companies learned, made steps in their transformation journey and moved ahead of their respective industries. The role of senior management is to build strategy, experimentation and execution into the day-to-day routines of the organization.

The consequence for the knowledge enterprise is that it will have to deal increasingly with different organizational logics at the same time. The streamlining strategy will tend to be more important in future years. For example, at the larger companies, orchestration has accelerated the introduction of collaboration and open campus and venturing systems. The systems are no longer the formal corset used to force groups with conflicting interests to cooperate. Instead, they are the tools for organizational units to steer themselves. High Tech Campus Eindhoven, DSM, Newtricious and Janssen Pharmaceutical companies have chosen to integrate the R&D function in a campus model with global reach. They have chosen not to steer R&D activities bureaucratically from one central point, but rather to challenge the business to shift its boundaries. The past five-year period can be characterized by a change of the business model and a change in the strategic roadmaps. The key driver is the movement to get closer to the market: "downscaling," "change to a market-oriented corporation," the "customer connection." Today, with a large number of firms having made much progress in streamlining their organization, innovation has started to gain a valuable new dimension: customer centricity and engagement. Open innovation and collaboration beyond the organizational boundaries is the true step ahead. Orchestration might be regarded in this respect as a new style of managing the benefits of hedging, streamlining and an open, collaborative innovation strategy; a consciously chosen strategy aimed at customer engagement.

References

Almiral, E. and Wareham, J. (2011). Living labs: Arbiters of mid and ground-level innovation, *Technology Analysis & Strategic Management*, 23(1), January 2011, 87–102.

Amit, R. and Zott, C. (2012). Creating value through business model innovation, *MIT Sloan Management Review*, Spring, March, 53(3), 41–49.

Anthony, S.D., Eyring, M. and Gibson, L. (2006). Mapping your innovation strategy, *Harvard Business Review*, May, 104–113.

Balogun, J. and Jenkins, M. (2003). Re-conceiving change management: A knowledge-based perspective, *European Management Journal*, 21(2) 247–257.

Banholzer, W.F. (2010). Creating value in turbulent times, *Research-Technology Management*, 53(1), 23–28.

Bell, K. (2012). Former Ritz Carlton president Horst Schulze Talks about the new frontier in luxury hotels, *Forbes*, 3 February.

Binns, A.J, Harreld, B., O'Reilly III, C. and Tushman, M.L. (2014). The art of strategic renewal, *Sloan Management Review*, 19 December, 8–9.

Birkinshaw, J., Bouguet, C. and Barsoux, J.L. (2011). The 5 myths of innovation, *MIT Sloan Management Review*, 52(2), 43–50.

Chandler, A.D. (1962). *Strategy and Structure: Chapters in the History of the Industrial Enterprise*, Cambridge, MA: MIT Press.

Chesbrough, H. (2003). *Open Innovation. The New Imperative For Creating and Profiting from Technology*, Boston: Harvard Business School Publishing.

Chesbrough, H. (2011). Bringing open innovation to services, *MIT Sloan Management Review*, 52(2), 85–90.

Chesbrough, H., Vanhaverbeke, W. and West, J. (2006). *Open Innovation — Research a New Paradigm*, Oxford: Oxford University Press.

Christensen, C.M. (1997). *The Innovator's Dilemma: When New Technologies Cause Great Firms to Fall*, Boston: Harvard Business School Press.

Christensen, C.M., Johnson, M.W. and Rigby, D.K. (2002). Foundations for growth: How to identify and build disruptive new businesses, *MIT Sloan Management Review*, Spring, 22–31.

Clark, K.B. and Wheelwright, S.C. (1993). *Managing New Product and Process Development*, New York: The Free Press.

Collins, J.C. (2001). *Good to Great: Why Some Companies Make the Leap ... and Others Don't*, New York, Collins Business.

Collins, J.C. and Hansen, M. (2011). *Great by Choice — Uncertainty, Chaos and Luck — Why Some Thrive Despite Them All*, London: HarperCollins.

Concertgebouw Orchestra (2014). History. Available online at: http://www.concertgebou workest.nl/en/orchestra/. Accessed 21 March 2014.

Cooper, R.G. (1994). Third Generation New Product Processes, *Journal of Product Innovation Management*, 11(1), 3–15.

Cooper, R.G. (1999). The invisible success factors in product innovation, *Journal of Product Innovation Management*, 16, 115–133.

Cooper, R.G. (2000). Winning with new products: Doing it right, *Ivey Business Journal*, July/August, 64(6), 54–62.

den Hertog, J.F., Cobbenhagen J., Huizenga, E. and Bodewijs, W. (2000). Blending Words and Numbers: Strategies for Combining Qualitative and Quantitative Methods for Organizational Research, MERIT research paper, Maastricht University.

den Hertog, J.F. and Huizenga, E. (2000). *The Knowledge Enterprise, Implementation of Intelligent Business Strategies*, London: Imperial College Press.

Drucker, P. (1998). *The Coming of the New Organization in: Harvard Business Review on Knowledge Management*, Boston: Harvard Business School Press.

Englund, R.L. and Graham, R.J. (1999). Linking projects to strategy, Strategic boundaries between order and chaos in organizations, *Journal of Product Innovation Management*, 16(1), 52–64.

Engwall, M. (2002). No project is an island: Linking projects to history and context, *Research Policy*, 32, 789–808.

Ettlie, J.E. and Rosenthal, R. (2011). Service vs manufacturing innovation, *Journal of Product Innovation Management*, 28(2), 285–299.

Eyring, M.J., Johnson, M.W. and Nair, H. (2011). New business models in emerging markets, *Harvard Business Review*, January/February, 89–95.

Fuchs, C. and Schreier, M. (2011). Customer empowerment in new product development, *Journal of Product Innovation Management*, 28(1), 17–32.

Funk, K. (2003). Sustainability and performance, *MIT Sloan Management Review*, 44(1), 65–70.

Galbraith, J.R. (1994) *Competing with Flexible Lateral Organizations*, 2nd edition, Reading: Addison Wesley.

Govindarajan, V. and Trimble, C. (2004). Strategic innovation and the science of learning, *MIT Sloan Management Review*, Winter, 67–75.

Gulati, R., Nohria, N. and Wohlgezogen, F. (2010). Roaring out of recession, *Harvard Business Review*, March, 63–69.

Gulati, R. and Oldroyd, J.B. (2005). The quest for customer focus, *Harvard Business Review*, April, 92–101.

Hamel, G. and Prahalad, C.K. (1990). *The Core Competence of the Corporation*, New York: Harvard Business School Press.

Hamel, G. and Prahalad, C.K. (1994). *Competing for the Future*, Boston: Harvard Business School Press.

Hoegl, M. and Gemuenden, H.G. (2001). Teamwork quality and the success of innovative projects: A theoretical concept and empirical evidence, *Organization Science*, 12(4), 435–449.

Huizenga, E. (2004). *Innovation Management in the ICT Sector: How Frontrunners Stay Ahead*, Cheltenham: Edward Elgar Publishing.

Huston, L. and Sakkab, N. (2006). Connect and develop: Inside Procter & Gamble's new model for innovation, *Harvard Business Review*, March, 58–66.

Immelt, J.R., Govindarajan, V. and Trimble, C. (2009). How GE is disrupting itself, *Harvard Business Review*, October, 56–65.

Johnson, M.W., Christensen, C.M. and Kagermann, H. (2009). Reinventing your business model, *Harvard Business Review*, December, 51–59.

Kamoche, K., Cunha, M.P.E. and da Cunha, J.V. (2003). Towards a theory of organizational improvisation: Looking beyond the jazz metaphor, *Journal of Management Studies*, 40, 2023–2051

Kim, W.C. and Mauborgne, R. (2009.) How strategy shapes structure, *Harvard Business Review*, September, 73–80.

Kirschbaum, R. (2005). *Open Innovation in Practice*, DSM publication.

Lawrence, P.R. and Lorsch, J.W. (1967). *Organization and Environment: Managing Differentiation and Integration*, New York: Harvard Business School Press.

Leonard-Barton, D. (1995). *Wellsprings of Knowledge*, New York: Harvard Business School Press.

Leenders, M. and Wierenga, B. (2008). The effect of the marketing — R&D interface on new product performance: The critical role of resources and scope, *International Journal of Research in Marketing*, 25, 56–68.

Lencioni, P. (2002). *Five Dysfunctions of Team*, New York: Jossey-Bass.

Lowell, B. and Farrell, D. (2008). Leading through uncertainty, *McKinsey Quarterly*, Issue 1.

Lynn, G.S., Skov, R.B. and Abel, K.D. (1999). Practices that support team learning and their impact on speed to market and new product success, *Journal of Product Innovation Management*, 16, 439–454.

Magretta, J. (2001). Why business models matter, *Harvard Business Review*, 80, May, 86–92.

McDonough III, E.F. (2001). An investigation of factors contributing to the success of cross-functional teams, *Journal of Product Innovation Management*, 17, 221–235.

Mintzberg, H. (1979). *The Structuring of Organizations*, New York: Prentrice Hall.

Mintzberg, H. (1990). "Strategy Formation: Schools of Thought," in Frederickson, J.W., ed., *Perspectives on Strategic Management*, New York: Harper Business, pp. 105–235.

Nagji, B. and Tuff, G. (2012). Managing your innovation portfolio, *Harvard Business Review*, May, 67–74.

Nijssen, E.J., Hillebrand, B., Vermeulen, A.M. and Kemp, R.G.M. (2006). Exploring product and service innovation similarities and differences, *International Journal of Research in Marketing*, 23, 241–251.

Nonaka, I. (1994). A dynamic theory of organizational knowledge creation, *Organization Science*, 5(1), 140–148.

Nonaka, I. and Takeuchi, H. (1996). *The Knowledge Creating Company*, Oxford: Oxford University Press.

Normann, R. (2001). *Reframing Business: When the Map Changes the Landscape*, Chichester: Wiley.

Nunes, P. and Breene, T. (2011). Reinvent your business before it's too late, *Harvard Business Review*, January/February, 80–87.

O'Reilly III, C.A. and Tushman, M.L. (2004). The ambidextrous organization, *Harvard Business Review*, April, 82(4), 74–81.

Parmar, R., Mackenzie, I., Cohn, D. and Gann, D. (2014). The new patterns of innovation, *Harvard Business Review*, January/February, 2–10.

Peters, T. and Waterman, R.H. (1982). *In Search of Excellence*, New York: Harper & Row.

Porter, M. (1985). *Competitive Advantage: Creating and Sustaining Superior Performance*, New York: The Free Press.

Prahalad, C.K. and Ramaswamy, V. (2000). Co-opting customer competence, *Harvard Business Review*, 78(1), 79–87.

Quinn, J.B. (1999). Strategic outsourcing: Leveraging knowledge capabilities, *Sloan Management Review*, 40, Summer, 9–21.

Rawson, A., Duncan, E. and Jones, C. (2013). The truth about customer experience: Touchpoints matter, but it's the full journey that really counts, *Harvard Business Review*, September, 2–10.

Rhodes, D. and Stelter, D. (2009). Seize advantage in a downturn. *Harvard Business Review*, February, 50–58.

Rigby, P.K., Gruver, K. and Allen, J. (2009). Innovation in turbulent times, *Harvard Business Review*, June, 79–86.

Ritz-Carlton (2014). Gold Standards. Available online at: http://corporate.ritzcarlton.com/en/About/GoldStandards.htm. Accessed 25 April 2014.

Rook, D. and Torbert, W.R. (2005). Seven Transformations of Leadership, *Harvard Business Review*, April, 67–76.

Rothaermel, F.T. and Hess, A.M. (2010). Innovation strategies combined, *MIT Sloan Management Review*, 51(3), 13–15.

Roussel, P.A., Saad, K.N. and Erickson, T.J. (1991). *The Third R&D Generation, Managing the Link to Corporate Strategy*, Boston: Harvard Business School Press.

Sawhney, M. and Parikh, D. (2001). Where value lives in a networked world, *Harvard Business Review*, January, 79–86.

Scharmer, O.C. (2009). *Theory U — Learning from the Future as It Emerges*, San Francisco: Berrett-Koehler Publishers.

Scharmer, O.C. and Kaufer, K. (2013). *Leading from the Emerging Future: From Ego-system to Ecosystem Economies*, San Francisco: Berrett-Koehler Publishers.

Senge, P. (1990). *The Fifth Discipline: The Art and Practice of the Learning Organization*, London: Century Business.

Shaprio, G. (2013). *Ninja Innovation: The Ten Killer Strategies of the World's Most Successful Businesses*, New York: HarperCollins.

Sorck, J. and Hill, P.A. (2000). Knowledge diffusion through "Strategic Communities", *Sloan Management Review*, 41(2), 62–74.

Sull, D. (2009). How to thrive in turbulent markets, *Harvard Business Review*, February, 78–88.

Stacey, R. (1996). *Strategic Management & Organizational Dynamics*, London: Pitman.

Takeuchi, H. and Nonaka, I. (1986). The new product development game: Stop running he relay race and take up rugby, *Harvard Business Review*, 64(1), 61–64.

Tidd, J., ed. (2004). *Service Innovation: Organizational responses to technological opportunities and market imperatives*, London: Imperial College Press.

Tushman, M.L. and Moore, W.L. (1988). *Readings in the management of innovation*, New York: Harper Business.

Ulwick, A.W. (2002). Turn customer input into innovation, *Harvard Business Review*, 90, January, 91–97.

van Leen, R. (2010). Innovation is in our genes: How DSM transformed itself through innovation, *PDMA Visions Magazine*, December, 14–17.

Volberda. H., Van den Bosch, F. and Heij, K. (2013). Re-inventing Business: How Companies Innovate their Business Model (*Re-inventing Business — Hoe bedrijven hun businessmodel innoveren*), Assen: Van Gorcum.

von Hippel, E. (1988). *The Sources of Innovation*, New York: Oxford University Press.

Yin, R.K. (1989). *Case Study Research, Design and Methods*, Beverly Hills: Sage.

Zaltman, G. (2003). *How Customers Think: Essential Insights into the Mind of the Market*, Boston: Harvard Business School Press.

Zook, C. (2007). Finding your next core business, *Harvard Business Review*, April, 66–75.

Zott, C. and Amit, R. (2008). The fit between product market strategy and business model: Implications for firm performance, *Strategic Management Journal*, 29(1), January, 1–26.

Index